IMAGINING GOD

Also by Trevor Dennis and published by SPCK

Speaking of God: A Collection of Stories (*Triangle*)
Sarah Laughed: Women's Voices in the Old Testament

IMAGINING GOD ~ Stories from Creation to Heaven

TREVOR DENNIS

First published in Great Britain 1997
Society for Promoting Christian Knowledge
Holy Trinity Church
Marylebone Road
London NW1 4DU

Biblical quotations are from the *New Revised Standard
Version* of the Bible © 1989.

British Library Cataloguing-in-Publication Data

A catalogue record of this book is available from
the British Library

ISBN 0–281–05040–6

Typeset by Wilmaset Ltd, Birkenhead, Wirral
Printed in Great Britain by
Biddles Ltd, Guildford and King's Lynn

CONTENTS

Introduction   1
 1 Child's Play   4
 2 God's Delight   8
 3 The Flood   11
 4 The Burning Bush   15
 5 What Hope for the World?   19
 6 The Fall of God   24
 7 A *Pas de Trois*?   28
 8 St Andrew's Day   31
 9 A Child is Born   36
10 All Heaven in my Arms   41
11 Anna   46
12 The River   50
13 A Strange Coronation   55
14 The Wild Sea   59
15 Darkness and Light   62
16 Transfiguration   65
17 A Man was Going up from Jericho
   to Jerusalem   69
18 The Darkness of the Cross   73
19 The Other Women   77
20 'Mary'   82
21 Mary's Story, a Second Time   87
22 Ascension   93
23 The Free Spirit of God   97
24 Find God, for God's Sake!   101
25 The Great Fish   107
26 Whispering Voices, and an Ancient
   Wood   110
27 A Crucifixion in Heaven   115
28 At the Dawn of Heaven   119

Introduction

God is familiar, well known and very close, yet so many these days do not feel the warmth of his embrace. God is beyond our imagining, mysterious, impossible to fathom, yet sometimes, when religious people talk about him, you would think they were talking about someone who ran the shop down the road. How to convey both the mystery and the familiarity? That is the question and the task facing anyone who would dare speak of God.

As many are rediscovering, one way to tackle this is through storytelling, for the language of stories is both familiar and strange, reminding us of what we know, while pointing beyond. This was the way chosen by the writers of the Bible, along with poetry, which is storytelling distilled. They did not strive for definition. They did not construct systems of belief. Instead, they wrote stories or poems, and made God the chief character. Without their powers of storytelling, their skill in creating and handling poetic imagery, the Bible would not have come into being, and the great faiths of Judaism and Christianity as we know them would not have been born. God would have had to find another way.

This small collection of stories is a testimony to the power of some of the Bible's stories upon me. Like those in my previous collection, *Speaking of God*, they were written for use in Christian public worship. I began preaching through storytelling some twenty years ago when I was a school chaplain, but the stories in this present collection all date from the time when I taught Old Testament Studies at Salisbury and Wells Theological College, or from these past few years when I have been on the staff of Chester Cathedral. On a few occasions I told a series of stories within a single service, which is why, for example, 'Darkness and Light', story 15 in this collection, follows on so clearly from story 14, 'The Wild Sea'.

One of the stories was written for a school assembly, another for a school service in the Cathedral, while a few more were composed for all-age worship. The rest were first intended for adult congregations. However, my experience tells me that such stories as these can often cross boundaries between age groups, and that people of different ages can enter into them and find different things, according to their levels of experience and maturity.

The Bible is the most obvious source for most of them. They reflect upon certain moments in the Bible's narrative, upon God's creating the world, the Flood, the life and death of Moses, the birth, life, death, resurrection and ascension of Jesus. They make direct use of the details and imagery of the biblical stories, but employ them with great freedom. They may lay one biblical story upon another, and another upon that; the chronology of the biblical narrative may be changed; images may be taken from one place and put in another; the original settings may be deliberately mixed with events of our own time. The other main source for these stories, my own memories and experience, I have treated with similar freedom. Thus I have used my imagination to play with both my memories and with the Bible. It is serious play, however, neither casual, nor cavalier. In the Bible's case it is meant to help bring some of its storytelling to life, and make its imagery new and fresh. The Bible's writing is so astonishing, yet sometimes, because of its familiarity, we are no longer astonished. Those are the times when we need to have things put in new ways.

Underlying all these stories are my own encounters with God. Very often, I believe, I have stumbled upon God in the act of writing them, and they have taken directions I did not anticipate when I began. I have found much grief and pain in my God, and much laughter and not a little mischief. I have found a longing for intimacy, and remarkable mercy. God is always there ahead of us, with his forgiveness and his arms outstretched.

What will we do with those waiting arms? Will we receive their embrace, or will we fix them to a cross? That is the urgent question which these stories ask.

Chester Cathedral

1 Child's Play

~

One hot afternoon Adam and Eve, unselfconsciously
naked, sat on the bank of one of the rivers of Eden,
dangling their feet in the water. Eve picked up a flat,
round stone, stood up and flicked it in twelve graceful
bounces right across to the other side.

'Who taught you to do that?' asked Adam.

'God did.'

Adam turned towards God. 'Did you really?'

'Yes.'

'Could you teach me?'

'Of course. Watch.'

God stood up, chose a stone carefully, kissed it, curled
his finger round it, and, with a movement of his wrist too
quick to catch, sent it spinning downstream. It went
almost as far as Adam and Eve could see, then swung
round in a tight circle and came speeding towards them
again, till with one last bounce it skipped back into God's
hand. It had hit the water two hundred times, and had
left two hundred circles spreading and entwining
themselves upon the surface. From the middle of each
circle a fish leaped, somersaulted, and splashed back into
the river.

'Now you try!' said God.

Adam pushed him into the water. God came to the
surface a few yards out from the bank. 'That was level
ten, by the way,' he called. 'Eve's only at level two at the
moment, aren't you Eve?'

'You were showing off, God,' said Eve. 'You'll be walking on the water next!'

'That's level twenty,' laughed God, and promptly disappeared beneath the surface.

So it was once in Eden. So it can be still. So it is, on rare and precious occasions. But Adam and Eve complicated matters. They grew up to think flicking stones child's play. They turned in upon themselves, and God remained out of sight, beneath the surface. They did not sit with him on the bank any more. Now and then, realizing their loneliness and overcome with sudden longing, they would gaze out across the water and see the ripples he left behind. But these were soon gone, and the water would resume its customary smoothness, as if nothing had happened, as if he had never been there. The Garden had ceased to be for them a holy place.

So they went in search of one. They left Eden behind. It was, after all, too small a place, too familiar. It held no surprises for them any more. They supposed they had nothing more to learn there, except for getting to levels ten or twelve, but that was child's play, not worthy of their ambitions.

God followed them at a distance. Sometimes they could hear his footsteps behind them. Occasionally he came so close they could feel his breath on the backs of their necks. Very occasionally he sat down with them and shared their food and made the spot at once a holy place. Yet they were never satisfied for long. They would move on, hoping for more, yearning, though they did not realize it, for the days when they could sit with their feet in the waters of Eden, and push God in and hear him laugh, and marvel at what he could do with a round pebble and a flick of the hand. It had all been so natural then. Perhaps it had not been child's play, after all. Perhaps it had been God's play. Perhaps they were the same thing. When such thoughts as these broke the surface of their minds, then God seemed, indeed was, very close once again.

Adam and Eve did not stay just Adam and Eve for very long. They had been told to be fruitful and multiply, and so they were and so they did, until, no longer only a couple, they became a family, then a clan, a tribe, a people.

The clan invented what they called 'religion', and the tribe and the people set about improving it. God was still following, at a distance. He carried a tent on his back, with the centre pole tied across his shoulders. The clan and the tribe tried to organize him. They told him where to pitch the tent, and the times when he should be there to meet them. But a sense of direction and punctuality did not seem to be among his strengths. Too often his tent was nowhere to be seen, or when they found it and raised the flaps to peer inside, he seemed not to be there.

The *people* said the whole idea of meeting God in a *tent* was absurd, if not an insult. They forgot it belonged to God and that he carried it himself on his back. They decided to make him a much finer place, one that could not be moved, one that was solid, predictable, fit for a king certainly, and suitable, they hoped, for a god. So they built him a temple in the heart of their capital city, next to the palace of their king, and nearly as big, overlaid its walls with gold and ivory, painted heaven on its ceilings, filled the air between with incense and sweet song, and became very serious about it all.

God arrived there one day, when the people were so

engrossed in what they were doing, that they were not expecting him at all.

'Do you have balloons here?' God enquired.

'Balloons?' they replied. 'Balloons? Balloons are child's play. We are serious here.'

'Oh,' said God, and retreated out of the door. He had propped up his tent in the entrance. He picked it up again, tied the pole across his shoulders, and went back to Eden to flick some pebbles.

The first one bounced three hundred times, went round in three circles and had the fish doing triple Salchows. 'Level twelve,' murmured God. But no one heard him.

2 God's Delight

God was hard at work. He could not quite get the jump right. The poor creature kept on landing on its head. He made the tail a little longer and thicker. 'Now try,' he said. The animal tried. God clapped his hands. 'Perfect!' he cried. 'Let's go and show the angels!' So off they went, and they found the angels practising to see how many of them could get on the head of a pin. 'Look at this!' said God, and tickled the nearest angel under the ribs. The angel fell off the pin and brought the whole heap of them on top of her. 'It's a kangaroo!' God shouted. The angels were still in a tangle, and couldn't see very well. 'Look,' God cried, 'watch this!' And the kangaroo went leaping all over God's new earth, and the angels picked themselves up and went whooping after it. They jumped up on to its back and went for the ride of their lives. 'Good one, God!' they shouted, and God laughed and turned back to his work.

In the next few days the angels had many a ride and found new places to hide in. They swung from the swaying elephant's trunk; they tunnelled through the soft earth with the mole; they stood cheering on the ears of the cheetah as it ran through the tall grass; they kept fingers pressed on their lips as they lay on the silent wings of the owl; they slid through the depths of the sea poised behind the whale's head, and then whooshed high in the air, when it surfaced and opened its blow-hole. They found sitting on the rhino's horn much more fun than piling on pinheads. They had siestas with the sloths and real piggybacks with the pigs. The antlers of the stags made wonderful climbing frames, and if they gave each other a sharp push they could slide all the way down the neck of the giraffe, along her back and fall off the tip of her tail. They hid in the flowers of foxgloves and frightened the bees, they climbed inside the harebell and blew with the mountain wind, and they spread their bright wings and swayed wildly on the tops of the fir trees in the storm, slipping into the crevices of the cones when they wanted some peace and quiet. And when the angels next met with God, they were so overcome by it all, they could not find any words, but wept tears of delight, and then took up a fiddle and a pipe and two drums, and led God in the noisiest, wildest, most abandoned dance he had ever danced, so that the earth shook for their joy, the great oceans swelled high with pleasure, and the sky that evening at sunset put on her finest dress, and trailed behind her stars so bright, they almost shone night into day.

The next day God's hands were still. He was thinking. If only he could make a creature to share with him the angels' delight, a creature which could weep with them tears of joy, and sit with them, overcome with awe, and hide and play with them, and take up instruments of music and lead him in the dance. The angels were not enough, not for the earth. They were made of the lightness of heaven. They did not come from his bare hands, shaped out of the earthy stuff of the earth. If only he could make a new creature, an earth creature, but a creature who would understand, who would know, who would love, as the angels did.

God thought for a long time, and then he knelt down

upon the ground and began to work. It took him a long time, but in the end he straightened his back, kissed them into life, and held them tight until their legs became steady. And still he held them tight, for he did not want to let them go. He knew, you see, what he had made. But eventually he released them from his arms, and taking them by the hand led them to the angels. And that is how, so this story goes, human beings first came upon the earth.

When the angels saw them, they were amazed. 'Now,' they said to God, 'you will have a creature of the earth to join with us and share your delight.' And the angels were right, partly. Partly, only partly. For, you see, as human beings spread across the earth, and became more and more powerful, and more and more clever, they forgot what the angels always remembered. They forgot that it was God's earth, and most of them did not play with the angels, or dance with God any more. And God's cheeks became wet with tears of sorrow, and one day, at the hands of his angel-like human beings, his face, beneath a crown of thorns, was stained with his own blood. And the angels bowed their heads that day, and hid their faces in their wings, and the earth shuddered, and the oceans roared in anger, and the sky became as black as death.

But that was not the end of the story. At the dawn of the third day God danced his wild dance again, and now, now the story has reached us. God stretches out his hands to us, and bids us join him in the dance of earth, while the angels play the drums and pipe and fiddle of heaven. And if we will but touch the tips of his fingers, we will remember what once we all knew, that this is God's earth, and we are made to share the angels' delight.

3   The Flood

The animals were lined up along the rails of the Ark, looking down at the water. Their faces were serious. They said nothing to one another. They did not move. Even their eyes did not flicker, but stayed fixed on the surface of the water below them. They were intent on the prodigious task they had undertaken.

At first it had been a great adventure. The creatures of the desert had never seen such water before. Some of the smaller ones had got so excited they had fallen overboard. The elephants had rescued them by trailing their trunks over the side. Other animals had just stood, their mouths hanging open in astonishment.

For the first ten days dolphins had played around the Ark, and great whales had come and slapped the water with their flukes and drenched them with the spray. The nightingale had sung night and day from the top of the mast. Old enmities had been forgotten. The wolf had dwelt with the lamb; the leopard had lain down with the kid; and the calf, the lion and the fatling together had taken evening walks on one of the lower decks, after all tucking into their mounds of hay. The animals had sorted everything out, while the human beings on board kept themselves to themselves, never emerging from their cabins. The owls had said it was because they were too ashamed to show their faces, but the other animals did not know what it was they could be ashamed of.

The Ark had drifted on, and the waters had got deeper

and deeper. They had come to have a strange look about them. Days had turned to weeks, and the animals' games had ceased one by one. Even the sloths had been quite frisky at the beginning, and the kangaroos had been impossible. Yet even they, the kangaroos, had quietened down, and now stood at the rail like the rest, staring down at the water, saying nothing. The birds had been the first to realize that the Ark was just drifting in huge circles. It was not going anywhere. It had, or seemed to have, no purpose. Still the human beings had not emerged from their cabins. No one was steering. There was no rudder to steer with, no sail, no oar, no direction.

How long would this last? There was nothing to see but water and more rain. Even for the desert animals the novelty had long worn off, and they had longed for their burrows in the warm sand. The unicorns had always been the most sensitive of the animals. One night they had leapt lightly over the rail. Two faint splashes, and they were never seen again. A great sadness had fallen over the whole Ark. The nightingale had stopped singing, and his place had been taken by the mourning dove. The dolphins had swum slowly round them, but they had not raced, nor leapt, nor dived any more. The whales had kept their distance, or else had gone down to the depths. They too had ceased their song. The waters had become silent.

The animals had come to feel lonely, abandoned, helpless. How long would this last? Might it never end? Fear had taken hold of them. Even the tigers had confessed their terror one night, and had shaken uncontrollably for hours. The animals had huddled together, suddenly aware of how small the Ark was.

Then one morning one of the antelopes, staring harder at the water than usual, and listening to the peculiar sigh

of the wind, had said softly, 'I know where we are.' The
animals had turned and looked at her. 'And I understand
now why the humans are so ashamed and keep behind
their cabin doors. We are adrift', she had announced, 'on
the ocean of God's tears.'

A long silence had fallen. Then one of the cats had said,
'When will we reach land?'

'I don't know that,' the antelope had said.

The two ravens at once had spread their wings and
flown off. They had been gone for days, and the other
creatures had given them up for lost. But at last they had
come back exhausted and had given their news. 'The
ocean goes right round Eden,' they said. 'We could go
round in circles like this for ever.'

The silence among the animals had deepened further.

'Then we must dry God's tears,' the otters had said. 'It
is the only way.'

For days now they had been wondering how that might
be done. The humans were still shut up in their shame,
with no mind nor energy to do anything, unaware of what
was planned. The animals were lined up along the rails,
staring at the water, racking their brains to see what
might be done. How might they teach God to laugh again?
They had chosen the greatest task in all the world. There
had been none larger since the days of Creation had
ended. No longer did they think about themselves. No
longer did they feel lonely, abandoned, or afraid. They
thought only of God's pain.

'Sing, nightingale!' said one of the tigers suddenly. 'Go
to the top of the mast and sing your wings off, and tell the
dolphins and the whales to fill the waters with their songs
again, and we tigers and lions will purr as loud and as deep
as we can, until the old timbers of this ship shake, and he

catches the vibrations! Let us *all* sing, or purr, or call, or do whatever we are best at doing, and if we are not in the same key, it will not matter! The ancient music of the spheres will have nothing on us!'

The cacophony was *enormous*, and the most beautiful sound the world had ever known, for it was sung with such large affection and such fervent hope.

So it was that the rains stopped and a few days later the animals found themselves drifting slowly down the Pishon River between the banks of the Garden of Eden. The kangaroos were impossible again, the gerbils had to be rescued from the water by the elephants six times, they were so excited, and just as they fell overboard for the seventh time, there was a soft bump, and the Ark came to rest against one of the banks.

Thus the gerbils were the first to return to Eden. The other animals let down the gangplanks, and tumbled off on to the land. The last to leave was the nightingale. With a final triumphant and quite astonishing burst of song, he flew from the mast-head, and joined his mate in the middle of one of the bushes beneath the Tree of Life.

Did I say he was the last? I am forgetting the human beings. They stayed in their cabins, not realizing they had come to land, let alone that they were back in Eden. They had no inkling of what the animals had done, or of the great task they had undertaken and fulfilled. They remained bent over their guilt, while the Ark, taken by the current, drifted away again, and slowly left the Garden behind.

4 The Burning Bush

'When did you first meet God?' I asked. Suddenly it seemed a very silly question to ask, but if the old man thought so himself, he did not show it.

'I was looking after my father-in-law's sheep.'

'But you are not a shepherd.'

'I was then. For a time. Till that fire. I was deep in the Sinai desert. It was hard to find enough for the sheep and goats to eat out there. One day I was leading them along the bottom of a narrow valley I had not entered before. The sides were steep, and the morning was young. The track was still in shadow, still held in the cold of the night. Then I saw it, a bush burning. Except it was not burning. Flames danced right enough, and soon, as I came nearer, I could feel their warmth. Yet there was no smoke, no crackling of the bush's twigs, just the bright, warm flames. The fire burned, but it did not destroy. I could not work it out. Eventually I stopped trying to understand, and was content to watch and stretch out my hands towards the blaze. Then suddenly all fell quiet. No longer could I hear the bleating of the animals, nor the running of the small stream flowing down the valley. All was silence, like the deep quiet before the creation of the world, till from the heart of the bush I heard my name. I looked round to see where I was! Then the fire called to me again, "Look, Moses! Look!" I peered into the heart of the flames, and then, all of a sudden, I saw my people back in Egypt with that tyrant of a Pharaoh on their backs. They were being treated like animals! No, far worse than that! We look after animals. Nobody was looking after them. They were being forced into impossible tasks, all day, under the burning sun. They were being kicked and beaten into submission. If they complained, they got clubbed to death. If they collapsed from exhaustion, they were left to die where they fell. They were bent, hollow-eyed, half-starved. And they were *my* people. I had run away and left them.

'"Go back, Moses, go back!" the fire said. "Bring them out."'

The old man stopped. I waited.

'What did you do?' I asked.

'I could not move. I was rooted to the spot by my terror. "How could I do that?" I cried. "They will kill me anyway. I cannot do it." The fire burned even brighter, and the flames leaped to touch the sky above me.

'"Listen, Moses," I heard, "listen!"

'Hardly knowing what I was doing I went one step nearer the fire, and saw again those terrifying pictures of my people being consumed, only this time I heard them also. I heard their cries, their incessant coughing and retching, their yells of pain, the small moans of their despair and their dying.

'And I was even more afraid.

'The voice from the fire came to me again, more insistent still: "Do you see now, Moses? Do you hear? I see also, only I see all there is to see. I hear, only I hear everything. It is more than I can bear, Moses. They are breaking my heart. Come with me, Moses. Bring my people out from all this, and mend my heart."

'I sank to my knees. ''I cannot do it,'' I whispered. ''I cannot. I cannot. You will have to find someone else.''

'The fire exploded, and the whole valley and its sky seemed caught in its flames. The voice came again, and came like thunder. I thought it would destroy me.' He paused a long time. Then he got up, turned away from me, and stood watching the sun setting behind the hills.

'That was the end of my shepherding,' he murmured. 'Not with the thunder, but with the silence that followed it, and the low, moaning wind. I looked across at the bush, and it was burned to ash. The flames were gone, and their warmth, too. The sun was much higher by then, but the cold of the night seemed to have fled for safety into that valley, and the shadows were turned jet black. I could see nothing, nor hear anything for a time, until the moan of that wind stirred the ashes of the fire, and shook me to tears. I gave up my shepherding, then.'

'Did you go back?' I asked.

'I went back.'

'With God?'

'He was there before me. He had never left.'

'Did you bring them out?'

'Yes.' He paused again. 'It was terrible,' he said softly, 'but we did it, God and I. We brought our people to that valley, and to the great mountain that soared above it. We met God again there, all of us, over and over again. But that is another story.'

He stopped, tired by his memories. He looked at me, and in the pupils of his eyes I saw strange flames dancing, and behind the flames a larger sadness. 'The first time in that valley I only *heard* God cry,' he said. 'The second time, when we were there all together, and the people decided to make a fire of their own and create a more convenient god out of its flames, I *saw* him also. I did my best to dry his tears, but I could do nothing to stop them. Nothing. I do not wish to see that again. I fear,' he added, 'I fear I will.'

5   *What Hope for the World?*

Moses had settled down. He had married a wife. They had two sons. He had a father-in-law who knew the ways of God. Presumably he had a mother-in-law, also, though perhaps she had died. He had employment. He looked after his father-in-law's sheep and goats. Not much, you might say, given his upbringing. But it was a steady job, if a bit dangerous at times, what with the wild animals and the snakes. And he was out of the real danger, the danger of that murderous country where he had been born.

Ethnic cleansing they had called it. The immigrant people he belonged to had scarcely been born. They had been still in their infancy, a threat to no one. But those in power had not recognized that. Full of absurd fear, they had decided on infanticide: all male babies to be killed at birth; none to be left to grow up into soldiers.

It had not worked. They had relied at first on midwives to do their dirty work for them. The midwives, however, had not co-operated, and had tricked them into thinking the task was impossible. So then they had decided to get their own people simply to throw the male babies of those immigrants into the river. Let them float on the current out to sea. To hell with the pollution! But that had not worked either. Those immigrant women had been too ingenious. That is how he had survived himself. His mother, and his sister as well, had been too clever for them. Though even they, in their wildest, their worst and their best dreams, had not bargained for the tyrant's own daughter finding him and then taking pity on him. Her father was behind the policy of genocide, yet she, his daughter, had taken pity on the child. She had brought him up in her own quarters. He had grown up at the heart of it all, at the heart of that wicked regime, at the nerve centre of its tyranny.

Had some of his people expected him to topple the tyrant as soon as he was old enough, and seize his power? He did not know. But he was out of all that now. Well out of it. He was well settled.

Then God came and unnerved him. He was in the wrong place, he was told. He had more important things to do than shepherding, apparently. He was to go back. God told him that several times, and in the end lost all patience with him. After that Moses had no choice. He told his father-in-law he had to go back to see the family, to see if they were still alive. He did not tell him the rest of it. There was no need for him to know.

So they began the long journey, he and his wife and two sons. He was going back to the most dangerous place on earth, with the most impossible of tasks to do. He had to rescue his people from that tyranny, put an end to the genocide, once and for all. For him that was bad enough. But for his wife and children it was worse. In no sense were they going home. They were leaving everything behind. They were losing everything, except their husband or their father, and their lives, and by the sound of it they would not have those for much longer. They went, nevertheless. His wife found it impossible to explain to the children why they were going, and he could do no better.

The journey was terrible, but its horrors paled into insignificance compared with those that awaited them.

They slipped across the border one misty night, cutting through the wire, and somehow, by the grace of God, missing the land-mines. Holding the children tight, and whispering to them not to make a sound, they eventually approached the ghetto where he had been born. The gates were unguarded. He could not understand that. They stopped in the shadows to listen. Nothing. They crept forward right up to the gates. Still, silence. The dawn had arrived, but there was no sign nor sound of life beyond their own breathing and their beating hearts. They went inside. They went from street to street. They came to the house where he thought he had been born. They went from one end of the ghetto to the other. It was empty. All were gone. Had they left of their own free will? Had they escaped? Was the tyrant dead, and the tyranny over? Were they all living in nice, leafy suburbs, shopping at kosher shops and walking to the synagogues for Shabbat? He looked at his wife. They would go down to the river, to see what they could find out. They would still have to be careful, of course. They did not yet know what the silence meant.

The river was not far. As they approached, alarming sounds met their ears: orders being given, angry shouts, cries of pain, occasional shots, and a low, persistent moan. They dropped to their hands and knees, crawled to the river bank, and peered between the clumps of reeds. Across the water a train stood in a station. Lines of people, men, women, and children stood on the platform, while others were being herded on to the train. It was not a train designed for people at all. The carriages were cattle trucks. They were already full, but the soldiers were ordering more people into them. The sun was high in the sky now, and hot. The loading took a long time.

Eventually it was done, and the train steamed out of the station, leaving only some soldiers on the platform, a few railway officials, and twelve bodies crumpled where they had been shot.

He was too late. And where was God? He had promised to meet him, when he returned.

His wife, Zipporah, broke the silence. 'We'll have to go to Sinai on our own,' she said.

He did not understand her, but he did not know where else to go. They took the children, and started back. For her and the children it was going home. Once more they crossed the border without being spotted. Once more they trailed across the desert, and eventually they came to the mountain at whose foot God had once met him and so unsettled him. They began to climb.

'Why are we bothering to go to the top?' he asked.

'You will see,' she said. 'You will see.'

They came towards the summit. Zipporah took the children aside, and told them to wait in the shade of some rocks. Then holding her husband's hand very tight, she took him to the top and pointed to the plain on the far side of the mountain. The railway track led into a huge camp. The last train was unloading. Rows and rows of huts, acres of mud, tall chimneys with smoke leaping from them telling that the fires were hot. All this was surrounded by watch-towers and a tall electric fence. They could see the guns of the soldiers. From the mountain of God they could see everything: the piles of twisted bodies being cleared from the gas chambers to be taken to the crematoria, the body of the young boy twitching on his rope, the woman impaled on the fence. The people from the train were being divided into two groups. One line would go straight to the gas chambers.

They put their arms tight round one another and stood weeping. 'We are too late,' he whispered. 'It is all over. And God is a liar. Or else he is dead also.'

'Look, Moses!' Zipporah cried suddenly. 'There, in the line being marched to the gas chambers, right in the middle.'

'My God!' he said. He started waving his arms and shouting. 'My God, my God, my God!'

The line disappeared, and was gone.

Moses raised his face to the empty sky and let loose a most terrible cry. Then he sank to his knees, and tore at the dust.

Zipporah knelt beside him, and put her arm across his shoulders. 'It would indeed be all over, if we had discovered God up here,' she said through her tears. 'But we haven't. He is down there, with his people. There is hope for us yet. There is hope for our people yet. With God in the camp, with God in the gas chamber, there is hope for the world. There is even hope for them.'

6 ~ *The Fall of God*

Climbing to the top of Mount Sinai was not easy. He would start off before dawn, to miss the full heat of the sun. The people would be asleep in their tents when he left. The lizards would be hiding in the crevices of the rock, and the foxes and mountain leopards would be back in their lairs, the night's hunting done. A few birds would be starting to call, and the ibex would be getting restless, but otherwise the night would still be holding the mountain, resting it against the slow breathing of the stars. Thus Moses would set out every day.

The paths soon became familiar to him, and the coming of the dawn also, though each time it was different from before. He would rest for a time at several places on the way up, but as he approached the summit the strength would return to his legs, his heart would no longer beat against his chest, and a strange excitement would come upon him. Each time it would remind him of how he had felt those years before, when he had stumbled upon the bush strangely burning in the desert, at the foot of this very mountain. He had been brought up in a Pharaoh's palace by a Pharaoh's daughter. But he had had to escape for his life, had fallen from princeling to shepherd, and had found himself that day minding his father-in-law's flocks, with nothing else to do but play tunes from home on his pipe. Then suddenly he had found himself on holy ground. He had been letting the sheep and goats walk all over it! It had seemed a patch of ground like any other, when all of a sudden it had blazed with the glory of God. After that, all had been altered. He had escaped for his life, and he had found it in that fire.

So now he came to the top of the mountain, to find again that holy fire, that warmth, that leaping excitement, that laughter, that delight; and he would speak with God no longer with fear as at the beginning, but as someone might talk with a friend. Emerging from their tents far below the people would look up towards the summit, but they would see it shrouded in thick darkness. For Moses it would be all ablaze, and his face would shine with its fire each time he walked back down the mountain paths and re-entered the camp.

Yet one day his climb was different. He began as usual in the cold air of the end of the night, and he rested at his usual places on the way up. The dawn came grey, and still cold. Clouds hid the sun from the mountain. There was nothing so very strange in that. But he was surprised that he saw no ibex at all, nor any of the other animals he had come to know. Of late a few ibex, even a fox or two and a leopard had joined him on his climb, and had gone with him to the very top. But this time they were nowhere to be seen. And no birds sang either. The dawn came and went in complete silence. The mountain seemed empty. Only the sky above it was full, as vast numbers of vultures flapped in high circles, waiting. Moses had never seen so many flying together before, nor so early in the day. They usually waited for the sun to warm the air and make the thermals for their wings to catch.

Strangest of all, as he neared the summit, his heart began to beat wildly, his legs would hardly move, and terror filled him. He crawled the last few yards on his hands and knees, and slumped exhausted on the ground. It was empty! The summit was empty! There was no delight, no fire, no warmth, no laughter. It was quite empty. The whole mountain was empty. Slowly he sat up. A soft movement caught his ear, and the leopard, one of the companions of his recent climbs, emerged from behind a rock and came and lay beside him. The animal was shivering. He put his arm upon her and stroked her ears. Such terrible emptiness! He did not know what to do, or where to go. He did not know how he might know anything any more.

They remained there, the two of them, for several hours, huddled together in the cold of the morning. Still the sun had not appeared. Then suddenly the leopard got up, her ears quivering. She padded over to where she could see the path that led from the camp below. She stiffened, then ran to Moses and drew him to where she had been standing. Moses looked down. Far below the people from the camp were making their way up the path. He had longed for the day when they would join him on the summit, but now he was filled with dread. The sounds of shouting and jeering came up to them from below. Then Moses saw him. The leopard had already caught sight of him, and had run terrified behind a rock. He was in the middle of them all, his head bowed beneath the weight of a circlet of desert thorns. His ankles were tied. His bare feet stumbled on the rough path, already bloodied by the sharpness of the stones. They had a rope about his wrists and were dragging him along, beating him with sticks as if he were a stubborn donkey.

Moses let out a cry that made the leopard's heart stop, and even made the vultures afraid. Its agony filled the desert, but the people did not hear it above the noise they were making.

They did not come right to the top. Some way below they left the path and gathered on the edge of a precipice. It fell away thousands of feet beneath them into a dark wadi they called the Valley of Death. 'No!' cried Moses, 'No! No! No!' He began to run wildly towards them. But he was too late. As he was running he saw two men take the bound figure and hurl him into space. A great cheer went up from the people. Moses stopped and sank to his knees. 'What have you done? What have you done?' he asked. But again the people did not hear him. They turned on their heels and started to go back down the mountain, singing a song Moses had never heard before.

He stayed on his knees. The leopard came quietly and sat beside him. Together, when the people had all gone, they went to the edge of the precipice and looked over. 'My Lord and my God,' Moses said quietly. 'My friend.'

7   A *Pas de Trois?*

I took him to a very high mountain. I did not show him all
the kingdoms of the world, but I let him see the Promised
Land, the Kingdom of God. Beneath us were the waters of
the Dead Sea. No fish swam there, no boats sailed, no
kingfishers hovered and dived. For myself, I saw only
death. But his eyes were filled with so many visions. They
had seen so many things. They had seen God dance, and
watched her cry. Now they looked down and saw the sea
as it might be, saw it as the Sea of Life. They saw its
depths alive with fish, bending, sliding, leaping bright in
the shining sun. They saw birds skimming its surface,
hovering, folding, plunging. On the far shore, where
barren wastes met my eyes, they saw valleys full of trees
or swathed with flowers. He looked from one end of the
land to the other. 'The Garden of God!' he cried. 'We
have found Eden!' He began to weep, and suddenly his
knees gave way. I caught him before he fell, and sat him
down upon a flat rock. Behind us the vultures turned on
their great wings.

'I must die here,' he said. 'I have come all this way,
and I must die *here*.' He looked a few miles to the north
and watched through silent tears as his people crossed the
Jordan river and entered the Land. His grip on my hand
tightened. 'My God, my God, why have you forsaken
me?' The words were spoken quietly, yet they were laden
with all his bitter sorrow and bewilderment. 'Over there,
in God's Garden, I could have walked with him in the

cool of the day! I could have shown my people how to till it and keep it. I could have reminded them whose Land it was. They will forget. They will forget.'

He watched as they danced on the bank of the river and flung the dust into the air with the stamping of their feet, and though I heard nothing from so far away, his ears could catch the strains of their song. 'I will sing to the Lord', they sang, 'for he has triumphed, yes, triumphed! My strength and my might is the Lord, and he has become my deliverance.'

'They will forget,' he said. 'They will think the Land is theirs. They have come out of slavery, but they will enslave others. They were born to oppression, but they will become masters of it themselves. They will spoil the Garden, and it will not be safe even for God to walk there any more. They will take him, and imprison him, and use him for their own purposes. One day they will kill him and God's Garden will become God's Tomb, and then the dream of the Sea of Life will die.

'My God, my God! Why have you forsaken me?'

He got up, and brushing me aside took his long staff, and strode with some of his old energy to the very edge of the ridge. He straightened his back. The rock fell away in front of him, dropping three thousand feet toward the sea. His staff banged on the ground. 'My God! My God!' he yelled, 'My God! Why have you abandoned me? Why?' Three more times his staff hit the ground: '*Why? Why? Why?*' High above him the vultures turned again, and a lone falcon pierced the sky with its sharp call.

Beneath its echo a deep silence fell upon the mountain. Moses knew that silence. It was not the silence of the desert. Nor was it the silence of death. It was the very silence of God. Many times he had heard it before. He wrapped his cloak about him and raised his head.

'Oh my friend, my friend,' came the voice, 'my old friend, do you think I have left you here? Just when you have reached the edge, do you think I have deserted you, after all we have been through together? Do you really think I could do that?' The old man stood tall, to the full height of his youth. 'They have abandoned me also,' the voice whispered. 'I too am left behind here. You were right. You saw some of it. You saw me taken, imprisoned in their small minds, used, killed. Yet you were looking so hard, you did not see me at your shoulder. I am abandoned, too. I am deserted, left behind, also. They dance down there on the banks of the Jordan and sing their songs of praise. Up here we are left, you and I, to a lonely *pas de deux*. Come, my old friend! Let us dance again! We will defy them, and call it "Resurrection"!'

'I have a friend here,' said Moses quietly. 'He helped me climb here, so I could see the Land before I died. Let us invite him to join our dance.'

They turned towards me. 'Come, friend,' they said. 'Will you make our *pas de deux* a *pas de trois*?'

8 St Andrew's Day

St Andrew's day falls on 30 November, and thus on the edge of,
or just within the season of Advent, the weeks leading up to
Christmas. I delivered this meditation at Salisbury and Wells
Theological College in a year when the feast was commemorated
on the Tuesday after the First Sunday in Advent.

This is the time of not yet, not yet.

The stable is yet empty of human company,
the star is not yet risen,
shepherds mind their own business,
sages divine nothing unusual in the heavens,
and babies in Bethlehem sleep soundly in their cots.

Soon it will be the time for bated breath,
for a sense of the world beginning to stir from
    hibernation,
for a tingling down the spine of the soul,
for the feeling of being on the brink again.

Yet now is still the time of not yet.
Advent is barely begun.
The Dead Sea is still deadly.
No nets are spread from En Gedi to En Eglaim,
and the streams that flow there from the west
are still dry,
even in winter,
but stains on the face of the rock.

For the moment we must be content with Andrew,
and with make-believe.

~

Patron saint of Scotland
(one called Regulus took an arm of yours there, so they
    say),
patron saint of Russia,
the hero of those who talk so passionately
of 'bringing them to know Jesus',
Andrew, Andrew,
what a figure we have made you!

Out of a few stones in the Gospels,
tiny things,
not all of them precious, even,
stones that nearly crumble to the touch,
out of these fragments
we have made you a shrine
for you to be proud of,
for us to shelter in
and draw our inspiration.

All make-believe, of course.
You were not what we say you are, Andrew.
Like us
you found yourself still in the time of not yet.

True, like Moses
you went up from the plain,
where we live, also,
on the brink,
on the edge
between wilderness and paradise,

in no-god's land,
like Moses you went to the top of the mountain
and there were shown all the Land of Promise,
where promise ceases to be promise
and becomes fulfilment,
where trees fruit every month of the year,
where cherubim have sheathed the flaming sword,
where there is no mourning, nor crying, nor pain any
    more,
where wolves lie down with lambs,
and a little child leads all creation by the hand.

Oh, I know, Andrew, what they tell me.
Strangely you were not invited
to be party to transfiguration.
But then, Andrew,
storytellers deal in threes,
and four's too many a cloud of witnesses.
Yet still,
you saw over time
what that transfiguration distilled
into one awful moment of blessing.

What you heard,
what you saw with your own eyes,
what you looked upon
and touched with your hands,
that is what we long for, Andrew.

That is why soon
we will feel ourselves on the brink again,
on the edge of our seats,
on the edge of our despairing,
ready to fall into hope,

on to God's ledge,
into God's eyrie,
to be warmed again by her brood-patch,
to be borne again on God's eagle's wings
and brought again to herself.

Well, not quite that, perhaps.
Like your shrine, Andrew,
our words have become extravagant,
too ornate for our shabbiness.
For this is the season of not yet,
and will remain so.

We are left at Advent
and beyond
to take some warmth
from the brutal fact
that Moses,
who had taken off shoes at Burning Bush
did not go barefoot, (nor shod)
into Promised Land,
but saw it only from afar.

We are left
to comfort
in your being left behind, also,
Andrew,
while others went to transfiguration,
over the border,
to the place where promise becomes fulfilment.

~

It is good to know we are not alone here,
between wilderness and paradise,

in no-god's land,
in no-man's, no-woman's land
for some,
land not fit for man, or woman, or beast,
or God.

Above all,
above all else,
it is good,
it is very good
to know that God himself
is left behind here
with us, in this place,
in this time.

For the Christ child also
it is Advent,
and the time for him is not yet, not yet.

Most strange and glorious humility!

9   A Child is Born

Matthew's story of the visit of the Magi to the infant Christ does not refer to them as kings. In his story they are not kings but astrologers. In those days, and in the culture of the ancient Near East and the Roman Empire, astrology was generally far more respectable than it is now. And, as far as the Jews were concerned, the cleverest ones, the wisest ones came from the East. Nowadays in the West we tend to think, if we do not think very hard, that they come from the West.

Matthew does not tell us how many astrologers there were. He speaks of three different kinds of gifts, and from that we have assumed he was thinking of three different people. It is possible he was, but he could have imagined seven, or five, or thirteen. In this story there are four.

Nor does Matthew's story make it clear whether or not they were all men. The conventions of the Greek language meant that you used the same masculine terms to describe either an all-male group, or a mixed group of men and women. Matthew wrote in Greek. Whether he imagined a mixed group, I do not know. Nobody can tell. I shall imagine two men, and two women.

One other thing. If astrologers were respectable, Jewish shepherds were not.

The journey from Jerusalem to Bethlehem was not a long one. Just a few miles. They knew where to go. The religious authorities in Jerusalem had told them. In fact, they would still have known the way without their advice.

To their clever eyes the movements of the heavens were clear enough. The light of the stars, so bright in that winter's sky, was drifting perceptibly towards Bethlehem, and the constellations seemed to bend their shapes in its direction.

Slowly they moved on. They said nothing. Their encounter with Herod and his advisers lay heavy on their thoughts. They who understood the signs in the heavens, were trying to penetrate the dark recesses of human minds. At last one of the women broke the silence.

'I still can't work it out,' she said. 'We told them they had their new king. The king they had been longing for for centuries. We told them. And when we asked, they told us where to go to find him. Why then are we travelling to Bethlehem on our own? Why haven't they come with us?'

'What are they afraid of?' said the second woman.

'Can't you guess?' said one of the men. 'Herod is a king, the king of the Jews. We asked the king of the Jews if he could tell us where the king of the Jews had been born. For him two kings in his kingdom is one king too many. The place where we are going will have to be on its guard against Herod, I can tell you.'

'Oh, yes,' cried the first woman. 'I realize that. And I share your fear, too. But what of the religious authorities, the ones who spoke of Bethlehem? What of them?'

'And', interrupted the other woman, 'what about the people of the city? We stirred up the whole place when we started asking our questions. Everyone was talking about him. What has happened to that excitement? They too have been waiting for this day for centuries, battering their God's door down that it might come. Why aren't they with us? Why aren't there thousands and thousands on this road? Why aren't they running ahead of us, to see who can get there first?'

The fourth member of the little party had been looking about him. 'At least the foxes are with us,' he said quietly, 'and the cranes.' The others looked to right and left and up into the sky. In the unusually bright light of the stars they could see the shapes of foxes running silently through the fields, and lines of cranes were crossing the strand of the Milky Way. They were all making for Bethlehem.

The four of them quickened their pace, one or two of them gladdened by the company of the animals and birds, the rest even more conscious of their loneliness.

They could hear Bethlehem coming before they got within a mile of it. All the people of the town were out. They were singing, and the sound stopped the four travellers in their tracks. The procession of their song and the golden lights from their torches wound its way towards them, and soon they were surrounded.

'Where did you learn that song?' they asked.

'The angels taught it to us,' someone said. 'Or rather the angels taught it to the shepherds, and the shepherds taught it to us.'

'Shepherds? Where are the shepherds now?'

'At the back of the procession, but you won't recognize them!' and the stranger laughed and slapped one of them on the back. 'They're the best-dressed shepherds you're likely to see this side of heaven!'

The people streamed past them still, but eventually they could see the last few torches coming near. And there they were, three shepherds, dressed up as kings and riding on camels, singing the angels' song! They had never seen such a sight before.

The camels stopped beside them, and with that awkward elegance of theirs, sat themselves down, so their riders could get off their backs. 'Welcome! Welcome!' the shepherd-kings cried. 'We knew you would come, though we were hoping for more of you. Where's Herod, and all his important people, and the people of Jerusalem? Did none of them come with you?'

'None,' they said.

The shepherd-kings shifted uneasily. 'Still, you're here,' they said. 'We'll take you to him, and we'll teach you the song on the way, so you can sing it to him as well, when you get there. And after you've been with him a while, we'll teach you and everyone else the angels' dance. The foxes and the cranes know it already, but we haven't taught it to the people yet. We were waiting for you.'

The procession turned about, reformed itself, and took its light and music back to the town and the child who had been born there. In the central square a young couple waited for them. A baby, wrapped warm against the night's cold, lay asleep in the woman's arms. The lights of the torches ringed them round, and the soft singing embraced them.

And so it was that the Wise Men and the Wise Women came from the East to Bethlehem, and heard there, in that small, unremarkable place, the angels' song, and found there, in that tiny form asleep in a woman's arms, the very love of God. It was much, much more than they had come for, quite beyond their wildest dreams.

'Take him,' the young woman said. 'He's yours, too.' One by one they held him in their arms, and sang to him their new song, and as they did so the shepherd-kings started a slow, rocking dance, and the people caught their

steps till the whole crowd moved as one. It was as if they
danced on air. Above them dawn came, and the sky was
full of cranes dancing that angels' dance. Between the legs
of the people the foxes bent and curled and brushed them
with their tails.

The fourth visitor had the child in her arms. 'It is all
heaven here,' she said.

No one could hear that other sound above the noise of
the singing, though some of the cranes flew off in alarm,
and a few of the foxes disappeared up dark side-streets.
Some way still beyond the town, the dust of the Jerusalem
road was being marched into the air by soldiers' feet,
enough to hide the Morning Star.

10 *All Heaven in my Arms*

On 6 January, 1992 I was in Bethlehem. It was not my first visit to the town, nor my last, but it was the only time I have been there for the Orthodox celebration of Christmas in the Church of the Nativity. Security was tight. Never mind its fame as the birthplace of King David and Jesus, Bethlehem had then long been a grey town, starved of funds under Israeli military occupation, and frequently under curfew. On the way to the church we were searched for weapons, and when we got to Manger Square, we found it dominated as usual by the police station, with its huge fence and its guard tower manned by two heavily armed soldiers. Inside the church, as we waited for the great procession to begin and the reading of the Christmas gospel, the police swaggered about. Not one of them removed his cap. It took me straight back to the stories of the birth of Christ in the Gospels of Matthew and Luke. They too speak of the dictates of an occupying power. They too speak of poverty and fear, and with his story of the massacre of the infants of the town by King Herod, Matthew tells of appalling violence far beyond anything (thank God!) we witnessed in the place. There is a very dark side to the stories of the birth of the Christ, which is there for us all to see in the Gospels, if only we will keep our eyes open for it. That darkness, and also my memories of Bethlehem (somewhat altered in the telling), as well as the common memory of the Holocaust, lie behind parts of this story. Thus I have deliberately blended together our own times with those of the historical Jesus, not just for effect, but because the story of his birth is as much for our generation as it was for his own. Time has proved its timeless quality and its eternal significance. I have tried to capture a fragment of that here.

I didn't want to go. But when she gets an idea in her head, there's no stopping her. She said she had to go to Bethlehem, and that was that. I couldn't let her go back there on her own. Too many soldiers about for a start. Besides, she insisted on starting well before it was light.

'All right, all right,' I said. 'I'll come, though what the point of it all is I can't imagine. All that way for some ruddy Jews.'

'What do you mean, "ruddy Jews"?'

'Bloody Yids, if you prefer! Bloody Yids! Always causing trouble, and if they're not, you can bet your last farthing they're about to start.'

'My grandfather was a "bloody Yid",' she said quietly. 'And he died because too many people thought him so. With six million others.' She slipped a bag over her shoulder, and went out into the street.

We walked in silence for several miles. The sky was all a-dance with stars, but I did not notice. Her grandfather was a Jew. I had not known that. Six million. I had been told that, but I had forgotten.

I was still caught in such thoughts when I became aware she was speaking to me.

'It must have nearly killed her,' she was saying.

'Who?'

'The child's mother. It must have nearly killed her. Nine months pregnant nearly, and she had to walk all the way from Nazareth to Bethlehem. Must have taken them ten days at least, more in her condition. And why? Because the occupying power said so. *Pax Romana! Pax Romana!* What do the Romans know of peace? Their precious peace meant she had to walk for days on end when she was nine months gone! Not surprising she had her baby as soon as they got there. A miracle she didn't have it on the way. She could have died in labour, too. She had nowhere decent for the birth. Only the place at the back where they kept the animals. And no midwife. Imagine! Exhausted, worn out after the trek from Nazareth, in a strange town, among strange people, no women friends to help, no midwife, in the cold dark of the night, and her labour pains begin. She must have been terrified. Her first child as well. And she's so young.'

'But why all this way to see her and her baby? We don't know them after all.'

'You'll see.'

We reached the edge of the town just before dawn broke. The new sun would soon rise huge above the mountains to the east and turn the round hills of the desert to pink and gold. The thin line of the waters of the Dead Sea would shine silver in the distance far below.

There was a check-point at the edge of the town. We were the only ones on the road, but the soldiers were very much awake. They searched our belongings, and then us. They were quick and efficient about it. They asked us where we were going. I didn't catch what my companion told them, but they seemed satisfied enough, and let us through.

The small square in the middle of Bethlehem was still quiet. We passed beneath the high fence round the police station. The soldier on duty on the tall watch-tower put his finger on the trigger of his machine gun, and watched us pass.

'Not a pretty place, Bethlehem,' I said.

'No,' she said. 'This way.'

She led me up a narrow street leading off one corner of the square. A cat slid out from one doorway into another. The silences of the night had not yet been broken. But then I heard a baby crying. New-born, I could tell. She touched my arm. 'Through here,' she said.

And there they were. The mother lying exhausted in the straw, the man cradling the baby in his arms, rocking him gently and singing him a lullaby. 'They look so young,' I thought to myself. 'She's scarcely more than a girl, and he's only a young lad.'

The man smiled at my companion. 'I'm beginning to get the hang of it,' he said. 'You've brought him with you after all, I see.' He turned towards me. 'You are most welcome,' he said. 'Sorry about his crying, but it's what babies do apparently.' He grinned. 'The shepherds woke him up. They didn't mean to. They've just left.' He began his song again.

I felt awkward. I didn't know these people. Why were we there?

'I've brought you some food and water, and a little wine,' my companion said.

'That's wonderful!' he said. 'Mary will say you're an angel,' and his grin spread even wider. 'Here, take the baby, and I'll give her something. She's very weak.' He looked at me. 'She nearly died, you know.'

My companion took the child and slowly rocked him till he fell quiet and closed his eyes. She held him tight against her for long minutes. Eventually she turned towards me. 'Your turn,' she said softly. 'Take him, and you'll find out why we have come.'

She passed the baby to me. He was so very small, that new-born Jewish boy, and I held him to me in the cold dawn, in a smelly stable, off a back street of an ugly little town watched over by soldiers, in a God-forsaken country run by foreigners who would make a woman nine months pregnant walk for days so they could get her and her husband on their wretched lists. And I tell you, at that moment I held all heaven in my arms. And when the baby stirred suddenly and twitched his arms and opened his eyes, it seemed, and still it seems, that I looked into the eyes of God.

Mary's voice came from the bed of straw. 'You know now why you have come,' she said simply.

I looked down at her. 'I know now,' I replied, and burst into tears.

11 *Anna*

Anna sat in the shade of the orange tree, her nephew beside her. She was all skin and bone, and the hand he held was tight with arthritis. Yet it was not her frailty he noticed, but the last energies of her spirit. When she walked she shuffled along at the pace of an exhausted snail. But her eyes still danced. That afternoon beneath the orange tree they were doing their last jig. Anna was dying.

The other side of the courtyard a small door led out into the narrow street. Soldiers passed up and down it at intervals. You could not go far in the city without finding soldiers, or without soldiers finding you.

'Did *you* sing him a song, aunt? When you saw him and took him in your arms, did you sing him a song of your own, like Simeon did?'

'Oh yes!' she cried. 'I sang him a song all right! An old song. A love song. My love song.' With that she shut her eyes, and in her quavering voice began to sing.

'Arise, my love, my fair one,
and come away;
for now the winter is past,
the rain is over and gone.
The flowers appear on the earth;
the time of singing has come,
and the voice of the turtledove
is heard in our land.

Arise, my love, my fair one,
and come away.[1]

Her voice faded away into the shadows, but the air still quivered with her music. At last silence came again, and she turned to her nephew and winked at him. 'It was more beautiful than Simeon's song,' she said, 'but they thought it too passionate to mention in their story. And they had to give him a bigger part to play, after all.'

'What do you mean, "after all"?'

'After all, he was a man!'

Her nephew shifted a little. She had spent all the sixty-three years of her widowhood, sixty-four, perhaps, in the Temple precincts. In all that time she had never been allowed to go beyond the Court of the Women, never been permitted to get closer to her God than that, for fear of her pollution.

She smiled. 'In the end it didn't matter,' she said. 'In the end my God came to me. He came among all those people, carried in a girl's arms. People thought I was nearly blind, but I recognized him at once. I saw him, and held him in these skinny arms of mine, and stroked his cheek with this gnarled hand, and sang him my love song, softly at first, but then as loud as I could. I woke him up. I woke my God out of his dreams with a love song!'

The sound of running feet, ugly shouting and then fighting came from the street beyond the wall and fluttered the leaves of the tree above her head and troubled its shade.

'What will become of him, I wonder? What will become of him, in all this? It is not the easiest of times to come to redeem the world.' She turned again to face her nephew. 'People thought I was a crazy old woman, who had married religion when my husband died, and been stuck with it ever since. Forgetting I was a prophet, they thought I knew nothing of the world, nor any of its dark secrets. But I know the beatings in dark corners, the people taken from their houses and never seen again, the children trapped in such despair that they try to get themselves killed. If I told this tree all I have seen and smelled of this city's fear and violence, it would shrivel up and die. Oh yes, I know. Why else do you suppose I spent all those years, those days, those long nights in fasting and prayer? Why else do you think I longed with such a deep longing for my God? There is such a need of him!' She raised her head. 'And now he has come!'

Beyond the wall of the courtyard two soldiers had a man by the hair and were dragging him off along the street, while others prepared the way for him with shouted abuse and sharp blows. Anna shuddered.

'Will they recognize him in all this?' Anna said. 'Only Simeon and I knew him when he came to the Temple. What will become of him? I will not see him again, for I am dying beneath this tree. Will they know him?' She looked straight at her nephew. The fingers of her hand unbent and gripped his arm. 'Will they know who he is, do you think?'

She closed her eyes. Her fingers relaxed, and behind her eyelids her pupils slowed their dance and stopped.

The shouting had passed further up the street and round a corner. In the uneasy quiet left behind, Anna's nephew could hear the faint sound of singing: 'Arise, my love, my fair one, and come away. Arise, my love, my fair one, and come away.'

NOTE
1 Song of Solomon 2.10–12,13b.

HK 29/6/97

12   The River

Up there, on the vastness of the bare hills, where the
buzzards and falcons spread their wings to the tall air,
streams well gently from the earth. When the wind and
the rain gather their forces together and hurl them upon
the land, when water slides in great sheets off the slopes,
when the sheep huddle against the fragments of last year's
heather and lambs die of wet and cold, still the streams
well gently from the earth. And when days of summer
come, when the warm air runs light fingers through the
tops of the grass, and larks lift high the earth's joy and
break it into song, yet still the streams well gently from
the earth. Even in rare years of drought, when the thirsty
sun sucks the moisture from the ground, cracks its face
and makes it look its age, then still, even then, silently,
without fuss, the streams of God's mercy well gently
from the earth.

And no one reaches their source, or finds from where
they spring. Only the curlews know.

The streams begin as they end, seeming without
purpose or limit. They spread themselves wide across the
high land, their movement imperceptible, narrow lines
hidden in the bent grass, clear-marked to the falcon's eye.

Yet the hills fold in upon them, lace them together,
bring them to the edge of their fall and send them
leaping and dancing among the rocks. God is then no
longer silent. he picks up his voice and roars his
laughter. The sides of the hills become his dancing-

floor and echo to His steps. The stream of His mercy
leaves behind the gentleness of its beginnings and shows
its power against the hard rocks, shaping them,
smoothing them, rounding them with gleaming hollows.
None can stop it. Oh, some come even there to try.
They cut channels to put it in their own directions;
they build great dams to hold it imprisoned, to keep it
in the places of their choosing. Always it breaks free. It
cuts new channels of its own, it bursts the dams, or
brims over the tops of them and spills like thunder
down their walls. It floats its spray on the bright wind,
clothes itself with rainbows, to refresh again the face of
the earth. It enters the woods of the mountains, and in
the dappled light of the trees dances measures more
abandoned still. It fills itself with life, and brings more
wherever it goes.

Beyond the foothills it finds a place for baptism. So a
man called John once discovered. He drew people from
the cities and the towns, from the villages and the lonely
farms, led them down to the banks of God's mercy, and
fair drowned them in it! With John they plunged in and
went deep in its depths. With John they felt its waters
embracing them, holding them, caressing them, and quite
forgot the need for air, till the warmth of the sun drew
them back to the surface. Some could not bear to leave
the water, but stayed in the shallows, splashing and
yelling their new glee. Others sat quietly on the bank and
let the water cool their tired feet, or lowered themselves
painfully into the water to bathe their wounds. Some,
coming to the river reluctantly, stood suspicious and
afraid in the shadows of the willows, not trusting the
strength of the stream, not daring to let go their hurt or
their guilt, or thinking themselves not good enough for

the general joy. They went away disappointed, and some never returned.

Some wished to keep the waters of the river to themselves. They could not stop its flow. They could, however, walk downstream till they were out of John's sight and beyond his hearing, to channel off some of the water into pools of their own. They could, quite easily, put high fences round those pools, and decide among themselves who might be allowed entrance and who might not. They could, each group of them, believe their pool was the best, and they were perfectly capable of despising the people of the other pools and teaching their children to do the same. They could do all that. So they did.

Until one particular dawn, when John, sitting alone beneath the oldest of the willows, saw a man coming towards him who he knew at once belonged to the river as no one else had ever done. This man came from the river's source and was acquainted with all its mysteries. He knew what the curlews knew and more, up there where the streams came gently welling from the earth. He could laugh God's laughter, and dance his ³ steps precisely, and he could himself refresh the face of the earth and renew its youth. With John the stranger dived into the water and went to its very lowest depths, deeper than any had gone before. With John, beneath the bank where the kingfishers had their nest, he danced and splashed, laughed and yelled God's glee. Again and again he took the water in his hands and hurled it far over the fields. One of the kingfishers, waiting on its perch to catch fish for its young, was disconcerted at first, then recognized the man and flew straight towards him, bringing him the light of the risen sun upon its back.

For a time and a time all seemed well.

Until in the laziness of the evening the stranger and John set themselves adrift on the river and let its currents carry them downstream. They rounded a long curve and saw the fences, and the narrow channels leading towards them. At once they clambered out on to the bank. 'They think they can keep the waters of mercy to themselves!' cried the stranger. 'Their pools are stagnant. My nostrils are full of their stink!' He turned towards John. 'We have a job to do, my friend!' They strode to the nearest of the pools and began tearing at the fence. They pulled down its planks, smashed them to bits, and broke the sluices. The people of the pool tried to stop them, but then the river, suddenly in flood, burst down the channel, overwhelmed the pool and all the others like it, and turned the surrounding fields into a lake. Terrified of mercy in such wild quantities, all the people fled to the higher ground, and watched aghast as the waters spread wider and wider.

Next morning, however, they recovered their senses. Groups which had long despised one another found unity in their hatred of John and the river man who kept him company. They began to plot how they might catch them and do away with them, and have the river to themselves.

You know the next parts of the story for yourselves, and you know also that other pools were built, and other stronger and higher fences put around them, and you understand that the work still goes on and that you and I have a hand in it ourselves.

Yet we know also, you and I, though sometimes we pretend we do not, that our work is not the end of it. For the river continues to flow, till it becomes a great ocean, where the whales sing and the long-winged albatross flies.

While up there, on the vastness of the bare hills, where the buzzards and falcons spread their wings to the tall air and the curlews call, the streams of God's mercy continue to well gently from the earth.

13 A Strange Coronation

'You remember me,' she said, 'though you may not recall my name. I am Mary of Bethany, sister of Martha and Lazarus. I am the one who anointed Jesus. I caused quite a stir at the time, though not as much as I might have done. Because no one understood what I was doing, not even Jesus himself. At least, that's what I thought at first.

'I first met him at the Jordan. We were all three of us there, Martha, Lazarus and I. We had gone to the river to hear John the Baptizer preach, and to be baptized by him. He was preaching about one who was to come after him. He spoke of that person as if he would be a king, whose reign would begin a new age in the history of the world. We didn't know quite what to make of that. But we lined up for John to thrust us beneath the surface of the water, and make us members of his new people of God.

'I was in front of Martha and Lazarus, but the man in front of me I didn't know. As I got close to John, I stepped a bit to one side and watched as he went about his work. But when it was the turn of the man in front, something very odd happened. The sounds of the crowd and the river suddenly disappeared from my ears, and there was a strange stillness all about. John clearly felt it too. He looked up at the young man, and began trembling. He was up to his waist in the water, but he made as if he was going to kneel at the young man's feet. But the man laughed and said something I couldn't catch, and John hesitated and then pushed him under the water.

He seemed to hold him down an age, and when he came up again, I found myself,' she paused for a while, 'I found myself in the presence of God.

'We were a religious family, of course, but God had always seemed in the distance. Once or twice I had caught the sight of his back as he went over my horizon, but that was all. When that young man came up out of the water, and turned towards me for a moment, it was as if I was looking into God's face. He and John embraced, and held each other, and then another strange thing happened. You will not believe it, but I tell you it happened. As he and John parted, a kingfisher flew and settled in the man's hands. The story got round later that it was a dove, but I was there, right next to him, and it was a kingfisher.

'I knew what I had witnessed. John had said one would come like a king. That young man was him. And what's more, what I had seen was part of his coronation. That's how I think of it, anyway. They used to take the kings at their coronations down to the brook Gihon outside the walls of Jerusalem in the old days, when they had kings in Jerusalem. And they used to talk of the Spirit of God coming upon the king at his anointing, and, it sounds silly, but I thought of that kingfisher, and I remembered feeling I was looking into the face of God. And I said to myself, this is no ordinary king.

'I never dreamed he would become a close friend of our family. His name was Jesus. But I've told you that already, haven't I.

'The ceremony, though, was not complete. I had witnessed part of his coronation, but there were bits missing. Where was the procession to the Temple? Where was the enthronement? Where was the anointing? You couldn't have a king without all those things too. John had performed part of the ceremony, but where was the rest? Would John see to it all? But then he was killed, and it was too late. The religious authorities didn't seem to be planning to organize it. Rather the reverse. Then there was the little matter of the Romans.

'Yet I couldn't forget. That strange stillness. John's trembling. Their embrace. The kingfisher. And that overwhelming sense that I was looking into the face of God. And then later his friendship, and Lazarus, of course. Lazarus. We thought we had lost him. We knew we had lost him. Jesus gave him back to us, and made the family complete again. That was when I decided that if no one else was going to anoint Jesus, I would. I would be his Moses, his Samuel, his Zadok the Priest. And I would do it with a greater love than they had ever shown to those they anointed. I would do it properly. I would get the very best ointment, and pour a flood of it over his head! I would *bathe* him in the stuff, and the smell would go up to heaven so that God would know all was well at last!

'I suppose it was a bit presumptuous of me, but Jesus stood so little on ceremony. I knew he wouldn't mind if it wasn't done by the High Priest. In fact, I thought he would want it done by a friend. I was right about that. The others there were shocked by what I did. I can't blame them. I would have been myself, if anyone else had done it. But he wasn't shocked. He was deeply moved by it all, and he kissed me, and wiped my tears and mixed them with his own.

'But he didn't understand. He thought I had anointed him for burial, as if he were a corpse. He said so, and I was so overcome, I couldn't say I wasn't doing that at all, but anointing him king. The smell of the perfume did go up to heaven, but things were not right.

'Then, the next day, I changed my mind. He *had* understood, for there he was entering Jerusalem with all the ceremony of a king, still smelling to high heaven from my ointment! And he went straight to the Temple as he should. But then it all went wrong, and from there it went from bad to much worse. They gave him the wrong crown altogether, and when he processed along the streets to his enthronement, it was terrible. He had to shuffle sideways along the narrowest parts of the streets, with a beam of wood strapped to his shoulders, and everybody jeering and hitting him in the genitals or the kidneys. I don't know how he survived that. But he didn't survive his enthronement. That killed him. Above a rubbish dump, it was, with two bandits being crucified along with him as his men of state.

'He looked at me just before he died. I was standing as near to his cross as the soldiers would let me, and he looked at me and said, "It is finished. John, you, Martha, and now this. It is finished."

'And once again, as on that day when we were up to our waists in the Jordan, I found myself in the presence of God, and found myself looking into his face. It was terrible.'

14 *The Wild Sea*

∼

'I saw it all from my graveyard. Everybody was indoors who could be. But I wasn't. Didn't want to be. Too comfortable indoors. I didn't want comfort.

'I saw it all. The sea can be really smooth when there's no wind, so smooth that when the kingfishers hover low for their fish, you can see their reflections in the water. But not that day. The sea had it in for him. I was watching him coming across with his mates. The boat looked very small. I watched it, and my fist was clenched tight. I was holding a sharp flint, and the edges began to cut into my skin, and the blood oozed round my fingers, but I didn't notice. I was watching the boat. I was watching him. He was asleep. You don't believe me, but I could see. The way he was lying in the stern of the boat. He was fast asleep. I could see.

'He didn't see it coming. Dead to the world, he was. Or looked like it. I heard it first. It almost knocked me off my feet and blew me over the edge into the sea. It was the wildest, the angriest wind I've ever seen. I danced with that wind! How I danced! The flint went sharp into my flesh and brought the blood, and the wind caught it from the wounds and blew it into patterns all over my naked body. I wanted to die, and now my time had come! My ecstasy was so great, I clean forgot about him for a while. But then the wind came with even greater force and threw me hard on to the ground. I lay there, trying to catch my breath. It was impossible to stand, but I managed to crawl behind one of the tombs, and from its shelter I looked down again at the sea below.

'I couldn't make out where sky stopped and sea began. They were one huge maelstrom. It was like that chaos from which the world began. I felt at home in it! I belonged to it! I had lived in it among the tombs for years. Now it had come to take him, too, and the world with him. I wanted to leap into the heart of it, but something stopped me from flying off the edge of the cliff, and kept me in my place.

'It was my fascination with him. He was fast asleep still. In the midst of that wild sea, in the very jaws of the storm, he was sleeping the sleep of a child! Or was it the sleep of death? Was he like Jonah, wanting to drown and escape God's whisperings in his ear, get final rest from his divine tinnitus? Was he like me, like *me* somehow, with a deep longing for death and the peace it would bring? No. I could see he was sleeping like a little child. The chaos was bearing down upon him with all its force, but he didn't feel it. In the middle of it all he was free.

'But his friends weren't. They were terrified. And they shook him and shook him till he woke up. I saw it all, though not quite. I saw him raise himself. I saw him stand. I saw him lift a hand. I saw his lips move. And then he was gone, covered, it seemed, by a huge wave and drowned out by the shriek of the wind. But it was the storm's last breath. With that last horrifying convulsion it died, and there he was, sitting quietly in the stern, while the boat rode the gentle swell, and his friends laughed hysterically with relief.

'I stood up slowly. I watched as the boat came to shore beneath me, and I kept my eyes fast on him as he climbed up the cliff path towards me. I meant to hurl my anger at

him for what he'd done, but somehow I couldn't find it in
me to say anything, and when he came to me and healed
my wounds, I, like his friends, could do nothing but
laugh, and call him, "My Lord, and my God".

'I don't live in the graveyard any more. Come on, let
me take you to my home. I've much more to tell. I've
only begun! I've only begun!'

15 ~ Darkness and Light

The man healed among the tombs had misunderstood. He had thought the forces of chaos had themselves died along with the storm's fury, that day in Galilee. He can be forgiven for thinking so. For his own chaos had left him, and for the first time for years calm and well-being had come and made their home with him. He was, as they say, and as they said, a different person. The lines of the flint upon him did not disappear entirely. Yet what he and others noticed were the marks of Christ's embrace. As the days and months passed into years, he could still feel its warmth, and those among whom he lived felt it also. It radiated from him, a more powerful force than ever his fury and his madness had been.

Yet he was wrong to think the final victory had been won. What he had witnessed on the Sea of Galilee was but a skirmish. The monster retreated to lick its wounds, and all too soon felt its strength returning. Before, when Christ had dared come on the scene, it had met him in the desert, hoping to catch him on his own, unawares, beyond help. That had not worked. It had mistaken the nature of his vulnerability. So this time it slipped into the city and waited for him there. It was not idle as it waited. It worked hard on other people's fears and ignorance, upon their greed and their narrow-mindedness. Their vulnerabilities were of a more ordinary kind. The monster could handle them, and knew well what it was doing.

It kept a close eye on Christ. Sometimes, as when he entered the city to all that hullabaloo, and went barging his way round the Temple, clearing the way so noisily towards the Holy of Holies, it was impossible to miss him. At other times he was less visible. The monster missed his anointing entirely. But then Jesus was the first of David's kings to have the ceremony performed by an unknown woman in a leper's house. The monster heard a whisper of it afterwards, but was not able to believe it. Nor did it know about the meal in the upper room, and those few startling words spoken over the bread and the cup of wine. Had it found out, it would never have understood, of course. As it was, its attention at the time lay elsewhere, with a band of soldiers waiting with swords and clubs for an informant to come and show them the way.

The monster saw him in Gethsemane before the soldiers reached him. His friends could not stay awake, but the monster could, and when it saw him sweating and heard the first of his words, its eyes lit up with an ancient glee. 'I have him!' it cried, and drowned out the end of Jesus' prayer.

After that it seemed to all concerned that indeed it did have him. Arrest, trials, sentence, execution; all, it seemed, went according to the monster's plan, everyone danced so accurately to his tune, and Jesus himself, under the lash of the soldiers' whips, appeared but a puppet jerking on its strings. It would soon be over.

At noon that day, that Friday, it seemed it was. Darkness fell, not the darkness of premature night, but the primeval black, the dark before Creation, the dark before Light and Beauty were made. It covered the whole universe. We may suppose that Calvary was sunk in darkness, while the hills and fields of Galilee shone with their customary light. But no. *All* was in that dark. The sun's light vanished, and the stars lost their light. The angels groped about in heaven, afraid for the very life of God.

For three whole hours that darkness prevailed. It penetrated to the depths of the deepest oceans, and out to the farthest galaxy. The creation was in terror. And just when its creatures thought they could endure no more, Jesus cried out with a loud voice, 'My God, my God, why have you abandoned me?' The earth and heaven shuddered, for it seemed that the heart of God had split in two. All, all seemed lost.

But the monster, hearing that prayer, shivered also. It reminded it too uncomfortably of the plain-speaking of Jesus which it had always found so hard to deal with. And it appealed too directly to God's mercy. At that very moment, as those words died on the wind and took Christ's breath away, when the creation was at the lowest point of its despair, the monster knew it was beaten. It could not destroy the love at the heart of God. Had the prayer been more cautious, or more polite, then it would have reckoned it still had the upper hand. But the words were those of one who trusted still in love. They were the prayer of the beloved to the beloved. Suddenly, for the monster, all was lost.

The Christ was dead, but light shone upon creation once again, not the customary light of a Palestinian Friday afternoon, but the Light that had shone out that very first day of Creation and which had so surprised its Maker. Only now it had a new beauty, one not seen before. Though only the angels and the monster recognized it, it was now suffused with the light of resurrection.

16 Transfiguration

~

Fleeing from a brother's murderous hatred, leaving behind a father cruelly wronged and carefully humiliated, victim of a mother's love, compelled by dark prophecy and driven by his own deceitfulness, sent to find a wife at a safe distance, Jacob, alone for the first time in his life, with no one to egg him on to further trickery, this Jacob found 'a certain place', and lay down to sleep.

There was nothing out of the ordinary about the place. No magnificent view, no scent of incense. Just a patch of ground like any other. So it seemed in the evening. By the morning it was different. By then all had been transfigured. Jacob had stumbled on the holy. 'Surely the Lord is in this place,' he cried, 'and I did not know it!'

That's how it is with the holy. We just find ourselves there. We find ourselves there. We find a patch of ground has become the gate of heaven, and in the most ordinary of places we find afresh the new-minted promises of God. That's how it is with the holy.

And is it any wonder that Jacob stumbled upon it when he was at his most vulnerable, when all his defences were down, when grand schemes lay all in ruins, and there was nothing to do but make the journey to an uncertain conclusion? Is it any wonder, this most remarkable thing?

~

Exiled by a Pharaoh's anger, leaving an Egyptian dead in the sand, victim of his impetuosity, driven by fear of arrest and execution, fallen from princeling to shepherd of someone else's sheep and goats, alone beside what he does not yet know is the mountain of God, Moses also found himself on holy ground. His flock, or rather his father-in-law's flock, were walking all over it, and leaving their marks upon it. He stood there, with his sandals firmly tied to his feet, playing a tune on his shepherd's pipe, thinking of other things.

There was at first nothing out of the ordinary about the place, nothing strange, nothing miraculous. Just a patch of ground like any other. But then, what was a moment before mere desert scrub became ablaze with the glory of God.

That's how it is with the holy. A flicker of time becomes, without warning, God's moment. A place, a patch of ground like any other is suddenly God's territory, and sandals have to be removed, and things are changed, and new promises emerge, and new demands are felt. That's how it is with the holy.

And is it any wonder that Moses stumbled upon it, when grand schemes seemed all in ruins, and there was nothing to do but lead sheep and goats from one place to another, with no end in sight? Is it any wonder, this most remarkable thing?

～

In a sense things did not change at all. The patch of ground at Bethel or Sinai remained a patch of ground. Yet no longer was it *just* a patch of ground. It was a place where things had been known for what they were, where truth had been discovered. It was a place where someone had had their eyes opened, and had seen with clarity, a place where someone had felt the touch of God.

~

Jesus was no different on that Mount of Transfiguration. There was no changing-room on the summit. He did not put on the glory of God. What changed was what his friends there saw, and felt, and understood.

So it is with the holy. Stripped of our pretensions, and of our striving, away from our cleverness, we suddenly see things as they are, whether our patch of ground be a falcon riding a high wind, or a dishevelled man begging at our door, a glorious falling in love, or a young man dying when (by God!) there should be life; whether, even, it is the bodies of three small girls pulled from a fire, whether it is the embrace of the one we have long loved, we see things, when a flicker of time becomes God's moment, as they are. For an instant we are clear about their worth, both realistic and astonished by their glory, and we glimpse or feel for a second the delight or the pain or the anger of God, and always the love. It is how it is with the holy.

~

And do such moments change us? Was Jacob transformed by his vision at Bethel, altered one jot by his wrestling all night (all night!) with God at the Jabbok? It does not seem so from the story.

Was Moses hurled into heroism by the sight of the Burning Bush? Well, he got there in the end, but 'hurled' is hardly the word. 'Protested', rather, 'squirmed', 'fidgeted about', till God lost all patience and gave him his marching orders.

And were the disciples themselves transfigured?

Golgotha does not say so, for then Peter, James and John were nowhere to be seen.

But that's how it often is with the holy. Too often we insist on returning to our blind stupidity. Too often we prefer crucifying God to being true to what we have seen and felt and touched.

Yet sometimes others notice it first - through the persistent grace of God, we are changed a little, and borrow something of his glory.

17 ~ A Man was Going up from Jericho to Jerusalem

It was a hot day. They were very nearly there, but they had walked many miles, and when they reached the far side of the Mount of Olives, they stopped to rest underneath one of the trees in a garden overlooking the city.

'What's this place called, Mum?' the small boy asked.

'Gethsemane.'

'And is that Jerusalem?'

'Yes. I've told you that already.'

'And what's that big building, all shiny in the sun?'

'I've told you that, too. That's the Temple.'

'What does Gethzebedee mean?'

'Geth*semane*.'

'But what does it mean?'

No answer.

The boy looked across at his mother. She had fallen asleep. He went off to look underneath some stones, to see if he could find something wet and wriggly. It was not difficult. Suddenly he felt tired, too. He popped the wet and wriggly thing inside a special little leather pouch he kept for wet and wriggly things, and went and lay down underneath the tree, near his mother. Half an hour later he woke up, turned over on his back, opened his eyes, and looked up through the branches. Four huge birds were circling in the sky above them.

'What are those, Mum?' he cried.

His mother snored.

'What are those birds, Mum? The birds flying up there, what are they, Mum?'

Another snore.

He got out his little pouch and shook the wet and wriggly thing on to one of his mother's toes.

'What? What's that? Ugh!' She jumped up in alarm, and shook her foot vigorously.

'You dreadful child, you and your wriggly things!'

'But what are those?' he asked, and pointed above their heads.

'Good heavens! Vultures! I've never seen vultures over Jerusalem before.' Then to herself she murmured, 'What death has brought them here?'

With their extraordinary eyes the vultures looked down upon the city, and saw everything. Soon they had seen more than enough. They wheeled towards the desert and the Jericho road. From their vast height they saw him walking his way towards the city with his friends. Bending their wings they dropped quickly towards him and landed in a rush in the middle of the road, just a few yards in front of them.

Jesus stopped and looked at them, wondering.

They shuffled their wings on their backs, and hopped in great agitation from one foot to another, making strange croaking and whistling sounds. The disciples laughed at their antics, and started mimicking them. Jesus himself was alarmed. He understood them. They were not antics to him. Then two of his friends got tired of them and ran at them, shouting and clapping their hands. The birds rose quickly into the air, and flew towards the Dead Sea behind them.

Jesus watched them go, then turned and walked on

towards the city, more slowly than before, and in silence.

They went on a few more miles, climbing all the time towards the hills on which the city stood. They stopped again. Down the road towards them came a young woman and a small boy, almost running. Jesus hurried to meet them, and they flung themselves at him, panting for breath. He knew them at once. They were old friends of his.

'Turn back, all of you,' the woman cried. 'There were vultures over the city!'

'I saw them first,' said the boy.

'Yes, you saw them first. I didn't know what they meant, but then we went across the Kidron into the city, and we saw everything.'

'Soldiers!' exclaimed the boy.

'Soldiers everywhere. They're waiting for you, Jesus. I know they are. I heard some of them talking. They're out for your blood.' The woman broke down in tears, and the boy at once followed. Jesus held them tight, till their sobbing came to an end.

He led them a little way beyond the side of the road. 'Sit down here, in the shade of these rocks. We've got cakes and oranges in our bags, and plenty of water. Sit and rest. I must be on my own for a while.'

He left the road and scrambled down into the wadi. He closed his eyes and listened. No voice came from heaven. No bush burned with holy fire. The desert was silent, save for the distant bleating of sheep and goats and the piping of their shepherd, and the faint calls of the vultures.

He looked down the wadi in the direction of Jericho. Then something caught his eye. Beneath a thorn bush an animal lay very still. It was a goat. At once he ran to it, his heart pounding in fear, knelt down beside it, and laid his hand upon its head. 'My old friend,' he said quietly, 'what have they done to you?'

The goat's horns were splintered, its coat torn to shreds, its side gashed with an ugly wound. The bush's thorns pierced its head. It was starved and dry-throated, driven there to die. Jesus fetched water from the stream in the bottom of the wadi, and moistened its lips. Slowly, painfully, it started to drink. He collected plants to feed it with, and its strength began to return. He covered its wound with his hand.

'There's no need for you to carry your great burden any more, my friend,' he said. 'I will bear it, now. I know the shepherd and his family down the valley. When you've recovered a bit more, I'll put you on my shoulders and take you to them. They're good people. They'll look after you. You needn't be afraid any more.'

When at last he clambered back up to the road and rejoined his friends, they were worried about him, he had been gone so long. The woman and the boy had left two hours before.

'Where have you been all this time?' they asked.

'I found the scapegoat. He needed some attention.'

He paused and looked up the road. 'To Jerusalem,' he said, and strode off towards the city.

His friends followed behind him, and asked him no more questions.

18 The Darkness of the Cross

When it was noon, darkness came over the whole
land until three in the afternoon. (Mark 15.33)

Then the people stood at a distance, while Moses
drew near to the thick darkness where God was.
(Exodus 20.21)

The small group looking on were frightened and
bewildered, as well they might be.

'What kind of darkness is this?' they said to one
another. 'What kind of dark is it, that descends at the
noonday and holds sway over all for three hours?'

'It is the darkness of the Creation,' said Eve, 'or
rather, the darkness that was before the Creation, the
darkness that lay upon the face of the deep, upon that
awesome *tehom*. It is the darkness of the world when there
was no world, but all was *tohu-bohu*, higgledy-piggledy,
topsy-turvy, here and there and nowhere at all. It is the
darkness of nothing, of waiting maybe, but only of
waiting. It is the darkness that was, before the Spirit of
God spread her bright wings over the deep, before the
lark ascended and called the world into being with her
song. In this dark the words, "Let there be . . . !" are yet
to be spoken. In this dark we wait still to hear God say,
"It is good!" In this dark of the Cross we wait for God to
break his silence and let the Word escape. In this dark we
sit and wait, and only wait.'

'Yet surely', said Noah, 'the darkness of the Cross is the darkness of *un*creation, of God's world all undone. It is the darkness of the forces of chaos once more unleashed. It is the darkness of the Flood, of the violence of the earth. It is the darkness of the human heart, the darkness of the fear of God's adventure that keeps us within our narrow orthodoxies, the darkness of our clinging on to power and on to familiar ways, and the terrifying darkness of treachery, betrayal, or blind brutality. It is the stifling darkness of loneliness and pain. It is the drab darkness of despair and the dashing of hopes. It is the dark night of the soul. It is the dark in us all, the darkness that envelops us all. It is, my friends, the thick darkness of Auschwitz, and it is also that familiar darkness which stops us seeing one another, and which lies in the forgotten corners of our minds. Thank God it is not complete! Thank God there is enough light for us to perceive, if we peer hard into this gloom, the shape of a cross, and just enough for us to see that the cross is not empty!'

'Yet wait,' said Ruth the Moabite. 'The light here in Israel has a rare clarity and intensity. What kind of darkness is it that can fall over Israel when the sun is at its fiercest? What kind of darkness is it that can wrap the whole of the Promised Land of God in its shroud, so that even the vultures and the night owls cannot see? The whole of this land is put in the dark of the Cross, and all is helplessness and bewilderment, all is not-knowing, all is waiting, all is terror. What darkness can it be that it has put out this sun?'

'It is the darkness of Egypt,' said Moses, 'the darkness of the ninth plague, the darkness that could be felt, and in which the Egyptians could not move for three days. It is the darkness which breaks the power of all sun gods, those of every land and every age. It is the darkness which denies all gods who seek to compel our worship by the fierceness of their heat and the necessity of their warmth. This darkness of the Cross strips away the pretence, the fine pretensions of those gods, whoever they are, whose work it is to make us feel small, whose calculations are inexorable, who go on their way unaffected by what we do, yet demanding our attentions. The sun does not enter into negotiations with us, nor into covenants of any sort. We cannot look it in the eye. It cannot be gainsaid. There can be no argument with it. It keeps us as children, longing for its return, or enjoying its warmth, or praying for some relief from its gasping heat. So it is with all sun gods. God defeated them in Egypt, and has returned, to Golgotha, to rob them of their power once and for all, and to give us back our dignity, our adulthood, our freedom, our responsibility, and our hope.'

'Yet still I wonder,' said Miriam. 'Is this darkness only the dark before the Creation, the dark of the Creation's undoing, the darkness defeating the gods who would keep us prisoner? Might it not also be the darkness of Sinai, that thick darkness where God was, the thick darkness where God is? Might not this darkness, here on Golgotha, be God's hiding place? Might not the dark of this brutal death be here to shield our eyes from the brightness of God and her love? Perhaps today God has come out of hiding, split the curtain of the holy of holies from top to bottom, and stepped out into the world, only to wrap herself quickly in darkness, to hide, not her modesty, but the fullness of her glory. Is God not concealed here, in this dark, waiting for us? You, my brother Moses, emerged from the darkness of Sinai with your face shining as bright as the sun, and bearing in your hands the love letters of God and her invitation to the wedding. We refused then. What might we expect, what might we hope for, what might we yearn for, and what might we do, this time, this Good, this Good, this Very Good Friday?'

They fell silent and had no more to say.

19　*The Other Women*

There were other women at the cross, beyond those of whom the Gospels speak. They came unseen by all but Christ himself, and only he heard their words, or felt them wash the blood from his feet with their tears. They were his last and most abiding companions.

Eve came, Mother of all that lives. Her name was fit for a goddess, and she came to meet the Christ on Golgotha with all her grandest ceremony. Her hair streamed out behind her in the wind of the world's first making, and her eyes shone with the light of the first stars.

Walking the hills of Galilee with Christ she had found again her ancient freedom and her dignity. With him there had been much work to be done. She was the Mother of all that lives, and there had been much death to defeat. But she had no longer had to endure the toil that had always threatened to bend her body or break her spirits. With Christ she had discovered her old courage also, and daring. There had been no cause to hide any more. She had been able to face anything, and face it she had! And with Christ she had grown wise. He had given her the fruit of the Tree of Knowledge, and in his hands it had brought not fear and shame as before, but delight, and power and new wisdom. She had turned into the queen she was always meant to be, and her merriment had spilled over the Sea of Galilee and made the fish leap.

So she came to Golgotha, holding the sun in her hand, ropes of flowers wound round her tall neck, and the jewels of the deep earth upon her fingers. But it was not as she expected. She had come for the coronation of her king, to cry 'Amen', to sing for him the love song of Creation, and lead him in the dance of Eden. But it was not as she expected. The sun in her hand went black. The jewels on her fingers lost their light, and the flowers about her neck closed their petals.

She had to change her song. It was still a love song, but not the one that had been sung at Creation. It was the song she had sung after the Flood, when all the world had drowned in God's tears. She had sung it then to console him, and so now she sung it again at the foot of the cross. And she laid the black sun there, and took her garlands of flowers and put them about his neck, and slipped her jewels on his twisted fingers. And she kissed him and wept.

Sarah was there also. Isaac had never come home. He had gone off one morning with his father, and she had never seen him again. Abraham had talked wild talk of a three-day journey, of fire and a knife and the building of an altar and the binding of her son, of how he had stopped and sacrificed a ram instead, and all she had asked was where Isaac was. He had not been able to tell her, so she had left and gone hunting for him. She had gone back to Ur, from where they had come originally, but Isaac was not there. She had gone down to Egypt, where once Abraham had so humiliated her, but they had heard nothing of her son. Christ had first discovered her among some tombs above the Sea of Galilee, where she had gone to see if Isaac's name was on any of the graves. Wild with grief, she had called Christ all the names under the sun and beaten his chest with her fists, and he had waited till she was done and could accept his embrace. She had kept him company ever since.

So she came to Golgotha, and waited till he died. And when they came to take his body down, she sat on the ground and asked them to lay his body in her lap. And so they did, and she bent her face to his, and said over and over again, 'My son, my son, my son, my son.'

~

Three other women were there at the cross, beyond those of whom the Gospels speak. The third was Job's wife. Mara, she was called. She had happened to be on the edge of the crowd as Christ had entered Jerusalem. She had watched the people as they had carpeted his way with branches of palm. She had listened to their coronation songs. She had followed him to the Temple and seen the mayhem he had caused. She had listened at the foot of some steps leading to an upper room. She had watched as he broke down in Gethsemane, as he was arrested with the kiss of a friend, as he was tried and tried again. She had heard his screams as the soldiers put him to the lash. She had followed him all the way to that strange hump of cracked rock above a rubbish dump outside the city walls.

All that time she had said nothing. She had not seen those moments when Christ had looked at her. He knew who she was, and why she was there. But she had never looked him in the eye, and she did not understand herself what she was doing. But when they nailed him to the wood, and the cries of agony broke from his throat and the fighting for breath began and the hopeless clinging on to life and its terrible pain, then she understood. She came out of the shadows where she had been standing, and she stood right in front of the cross, and called up to Christ to gain his attention. 'How long will you go on clinging to your innocence?' she shouted. 'Curse God, and die! Curse God, and die!'

There was silence. The onlookers stopped their mockery and waited. The thief who had been shouting at Christ for so long was quiet. For a third time Mara shouted, 'Curse God, and die!'

Christ's body twisted and pulled at the nails. He seemed to be gathering all his strength for one last effort. Slowly he lifted his head. 'My God, my God, why have you abandoned me? Why? Why? Why?'

His voice seemed to split heaven in two. A fearful darkness fell upon the place, the earth shuddered and broke apart, and all those beneath the cross were thrown to the ground. All except Mara. She stood there stock still. She remembered the time when she and her husband, Job, had suffered so very terribly, and she recalled how insufferable he had been at first, until the dam of his piety had burst and he had dared for the first time in his life to look God in the eye and tell him what was in his heart.

In the end his God had come out of hiding and taken him by the hand and shown him all the secrets of the universe. That, of course, had changed him quite. But Mara had not received the vision herself. There had been no Grand Tour for her. She had not heard God's exquisite commentary. For her there had been no end, no conclusion, only a loneliness and a bewilderment which all Job's new love had not been able to penetrate.

And there she was on Golgotha, and once again she had

cried those terrible words, 'Curse God, and die!' Only this time she had not been rebuked. This time the man had had no dam of frightened piety to break. This time she had been listened to, her words had been heeded.

Yet that was not why she was weeping. She was weeping because she knew what Christ's words meant. She had heard her husband shouting at God, beating at God's door with his own terrifying words, and she had not known till then that he had loved God so much, nor put so much trust in his mercy. Now, on Golgotha, when she heard Christ's bitterness burst from his body, she recognized it at once as the cry of the lover to the beloved. She knew the quaking earth was deceived, for there was no cause for fear. Christ had looked God in the eye, and shown him his heart. All was revealed. For the first time she herself saw the love at the heart of God. Her husband had told her of it, told her of what he had seen and heard. But she had only heard by the hearing of the ear. She had not seen, she had not known for herself. Not till that moment when Christ raised his head and bellowed out his pain.

She stepped forward and laid her head on his feet. The last thing he knew before he died was her tears mingling with his blood. He wanted to give her a new name, for Mara, 'Bitterness', no longer spoke of her. But he could not find the breath. It died on his lips.

Yet it would not be long before he would meet her again, walking in his garden in the cool of the new day. Then he would call her Mary, and she would find resurrection.

20 'Mary'

In the far distance the snows of Mount Hermon were turning pink in the setting sun. The waters of the Sea of Galilee lay still, basking in the warmth of the evening. Tiny waves broke a few yards in front of where we were sitting. Cormorants flew low over the open water, and closer to the shore black and white kingfishers dived for their fish.

I had come to Magdala to find her. She had returned to her home town when it was all over and become the leader of a small community there. She was an old woman now, revered by all the followers of Jesus in Palestine and beyond. Some spoke of her with awe. Some said she had been as close to Jesus as Peter or John. Closer still, others said. And there I was, drinking wine with her on a spring evening beside the Sea of Galilee! Mary of Magdala.

Our laughter spilled out across the Sea. 'We'll frighten the kingfishers, if we're not careful,' she said. 'See, they've disappeared already!'

The sun slid down behind the high ridge at the back of the village. Darkness would come quickly. She poured me another glass of wine, and we fell silent at last. Night came and filled the sky with stars.

'I was very ill,' she said quietly. 'You have been waiting for me to tell you my story. I can tell it more easily in the dark. The darkness conjures up my memories of him.

'I was very ill. Possessed, they said I was. By seven

demons. That's how ill I was. They thought I wouldn't live long. I don't know what the illness was, but it lay heavy on me. I felt shut in by it. I was imprisoned, confined to the tiny room of my sickness. It seemed to fill my world. There was nothing else. I was trapped by it, eaten up by it. It was a strange kind of dark, and I couldn't see anything else. You know what it's like when you're very ill. You can think of nothing else, do nothing else, be nothing else. I was cut off, alone, quite alone, afraid of everyone and everything, afraid of my family and my friends, afraid of myself and my bitter anger, afraid of God, afraid of dying. No one could reach me. No one knew the way into the small room where I lived with my illness. People were themselves frightened of me.

'Then one day he came to Magdala and walked straight in. He had no fear you see, and he knew precisely what he was dealing with. I do not remember much. I recall being huddled in the corner of my room, as I always was. And I remember him calling my name, "Mary". I remember him reaching out his hand to me. I remember his voice and his touch. That is all. Except for him bringing me out into the sunlight, shielding my eyes against the glare, and leading me down to the edge of the sea here, and showing me the snows of Hermon and the kingfishers plunging for their fish. He held me here, on this very spot - I was extremely weak, of course - and he opened my eyes and let in the world again. Only I saw it as I had never seen it before. He stayed in the village a few days, and by the time he left I was strong enough, remarkably, to go with him. So I did. All the way to Jerusalem.'

She fell silent once more. The small waves hissed and sighed in front of us. She peered out into the darkness.

'Crucifixion is a most terrifying way to kill someone,'

she said. 'I had seen it before. It wasn't new to me. But his death . . .' Her voice trailed off. She got up and stood by the water's edge. The waves curled round her feet, while she fixed her eyes on the blackness ahead of her. 'The words came from her firm and strong. 'They had all deserted him. All the men following him. They had all gone. No one was there, except me and a few other women who were also his close friends. They crucified him above a rubbish dump. The Romans chose the place carefully. ''The King of the Jews'' dying in slow agony above a rubbish dump. They thought the Jews would learn their lesson from that. They wouldn't let us women near him. We had to stand back from their brutality, but the distance was itself so cruel. We wanted to do for him anything we could. For God's sake that wouldn't have been much! But they kept us at a distance. We were helpless. We could do nothing. I remembered the tiny room of my sickness, and my isolation and my fear. This time I was afraid not just for myself, but for the whole world. It had gone mad! I was afraid for him in his pain, near to death. I was afraid for God. It was the middle of the day, yet everything seemed pitched into darkness. We found ourselves groping about for something to hold on to, but found nothing. I remember that black. It was worse, far more dreadful than the darkness which had so nearly consumed me when I was ill. It was as if God's own light had been snuffed out, and nothing was left but the smoke and the smell of his pain. I felt I too would die, and as what I thought would be my last word, I called out his name. Even at that distance, he turned his head and looked, and then he said something I couldn't catch. At the sound of his cry I knew where I was. I was on Sinai, and this was the thick darkness where God was,

the darkness Moses knew. Only I hadn't imagined it
would be like that, and I didn't know what to make of it
all.

'For a moment I had seen the truth, but a minute later
his head fell and we knew he was dead, and grief wrapped
its cold cloak about me and drew its hood over my eyes.

'We went to bury him, and I forgot what I had seen in
the darkness of his dying. I could not leave him. That was
all I knew. The next day, the Sabbath, was another agony
of waiting. I had waited for him to die. Now I waited to
visit his tomb. I was there before dawn the next day. I saw
in the dark the deeper blackness of the tomb. I peered
into its recesses, and it hit me with all its cruel force. He
was gone! It was all at an end. My world. God's world.
All over. Finished with. I was left with a terrifying
emptiness, and I ran with it all the way to Peter and John.
I told them and we went back to the garden together, but
they didn't spend long at the tomb, and soon I was there
once more on my own. The silence was complete, and
darkness still had the world by the throat. There was
nothing, nothing, nothing. I do not remember much. I
recall being huddled in my fear and pain in the corner of
the garden where his tomb was. And I remember him
calling my name, "Mary". And I remember realizing
what it was he had said as he was dying. He had called my
name. I had not heard him then. Now, in his garden, I
did. "Mary". I remember being then no longer afraid.
I remember raising my eyes, and I remember seeing
him, and, I tell you, it was the world's dawn, and mine
also. Then I heard the birds. They had been singing
for some time, but I had been deafened by grief. It was as
if all the birds in creation were in that garden in full
voice, bursting their lungs, and practically falling off their

perches in the effort! It was just one word that did it. My name. I shall never forget it.' Then realizing what she had said, she burst out laughing.

21   Mary's Story,
a Second Time

The sun had not long risen above the mountains to the
east of the Dead Sea, but already the night's chill was
leaving the hills of the Judean desert, except where the
fissures of the wadi kept the shadows deep. It was very
quiet. The only sounds the group could hear were the
playing of the thin stream at the bottom of the wadi far
below them, and the music of a shepherd the other side,
as she piped her sheep and goats down towards the water
and the vegetation beside it.

They were listening intently to an old woman. She was
thin and wiry, strong still, and as fit as many a much
younger person. Her eyes were as bright as heaven. She
seemed afraid of no one, of nothing at all. They called her
Mary of Magdala.

She would take small groups of people into the high
country of Galilee up in the north, or out into this desert
east of Jerusalem. They would leave some time before
dawn, find a place to sit down as the sun was coming up,
and she would bless and break bread, and bless and pour
the wine as she had seen him do, and then they would eat
and drink together, while she scanned the hills as if
looking for someone who should be there.

Eventually she would emerge from her reverie and
place her hand on the shoulder of the person sitting beside
her, and the questions would be asked afresh. Always they
wanted to know what it had been like being there as he
died on the cross, being there, three days later, to find

him (the first person to find him), close to his garden
tomb.

She never tired of telling it all, and each time she
would tell it differently from before. But then they would
ask what it all meant, and she would become silent again,
and gaze once more over the hills, or pick up a small
piece of rock and study its contours and colours. This
time, sitting on the edge of the wadi, she sat listening to
the distant sound of the shepherd's pipe, and watched as a
large kingfisher flew down towards the stream beyond the
flocks and flashed the early sun from its sharp, turquoise
wings. So astonishing in its beauty against the browns and
faint greens of the hills, the bird lit up her face, and
loosened her tongue.

'What does it all mean?' they had asked.

'I do not know, though that bird has made me a little
wiser. It will take the rest of history to work it out and
penetrate its mysteries, and even then we will only know
the half of it. But I understand a part of it, a little.

'It was a shifting of power, as great as the movement of
the earth that brought these strange, round hills into
being, and split the earth's surface apart to make the
Jordan valley and the Dead Sea near here, and the Sea of
Galilee where I live. I have heard someone say there was
an earthquake when Jesus died. I know what he meant.

'Those who thought they had power had none, and
those who seemed to have none held in their hands the
very power of God. Think of the power Herod thought he
had! Think of the magnificence of his father's palaces and
the Temple his father created in Jerusalem! Think of the
town of Tiberias which he himself built on the shores of
the Sea of Galilee! He thought he could have whatever he
wanted from Jesus. All he got was silence. He could not

take that. So he turned to bullying and got his soldiers to join in. Bullying made him laugh, but still brought nothing from Jesus but cries of pain as the soldiers hit him. Their cruelty was a sign of their powerlessness. Herod's places will one day fall into ruin, but we will still be able to hear Jesus' silence and catch his pain.

'It was the same with Pilate and the Roman soldiers who put him to the lash and later nailed him to a cross. They thought they were in control, and that the power was theirs. They thought he had nothing but an agonizing death. They did not know against whom they fought, nor did I understand at the time. They were doing battle against the very love of God. They whirled their fine swords and brought them crashing down upon that love's granite, and it splintered them into a thousand pieces. You can never break the love of God, never!

'My friend, my dear friend who hung there, unable to move, just able to breathe, able after a spell only to die, he held in his pierced hands the very power of God! The world had not seen such power since God created it. For when he made it all so very beautiful, and made us human beings so very good, he gave half his power to us. Some we used very well, and some we did not. But we had never seen the Creator's power, not all of it, not the power that brought light out of the first dark, put chaos into good order, filled the seas with life, and the sky with birds and their song, and covered the earth with plants and animals of every kind. We had not seen *that* power, for as soon as we were made, he gave so much of it away. Yet I saw it then, on Calvary. At least I know that now. I found out three days later. At the time I was blinded by my fear, grief and anger at all the brutality, my friend's agony, and the terrible, terrible waste of his life.

'I felt then that I possessed no power at all. I and the other women could do nothing. We stood at a distance and the soldiers kept us there. When he was thirsty, we could not give him anything to drink. When he cried out his abandonment, how God, even God had deserted him, we could not embrace him, or even make ourselves heard above the din.

'It was noon, you know, when they crucified him. It should have been the hottest, brightest part of the day, yet even the sun seemed robbed of its strength. It felt as cold as a winter's night, and just as dark.

'So he died, and we buried him, in a hurry, because the Sabbath was about to begin. We did not have time to lay him out properly.

'I remember nothing of that Sabbath, nor of the night that followed it, except that I could not sleep. I was back at the tomb before dawn. I do not know what I was doing there exactly, nor what I was looking for. But I know what I found. Nothing! And that put me in a panic, and I ran and told Peter and John and they went to the garden and I followed as best I could. When I got there they had left already. I was on my own once more, and there was nothing I could do but weep. I was alone in the tomb of my bewilderment and grief. It was, I thought, the world's end. Until the moment he called my name.'

She paused and listened to the shepherd still playing by the water's edge.

'I thought I was left with nothing. I thought the forces of darkness had won. I thought despair, grief and death were all that remained for me, and fear and more violence for God's world - only it was not God's world any more. But then I heard him call my name, and I knew then that the world and I had everything! I knew also where I was. I was not in the garden of the tombs, the garden of death. I was in God's garden. I had stumbled upon Eden, and found him walking there in the cool of the new day! He had called me, and I had come out of the hiding place of my misery. There was no cause for fear any more. All things were well, all manner of things were well. I had discovered Eden, the Garden of God, where first he had given us the kiss of life and moulded us with his bare hands. I wanted to embrace him, cling to him and stay for ever in that place, to eat the fruit of its trees, swim in its broad rivers, walk its paths with him, and, in his company, find all its surprises and its treasures. I was quite overcome with joy.'

She stopped and waved down at the shepherd who was now immediately below them. The girl stopped her playing and waved back.

'But I could not stay,' she continued. 'I could not keep what I found to myself. If you had discovered Eden, and heard your name called like that, out of the blue, and found him again and more than we had ever known he was, could you have kept that to yourself? Of course not. I walked back to the others, and I sat in silence in the middle of them for half an hour or more, and then I told them as much as words would allow. Eventually I returned to Magdala, and the other places round the lake, and now here I am with you.'

She looked round at the people in the circle. She knew them all. She knew their tragedies and the scars those had left behind. She knew their fears, and their temptation to despair. 'There is hope for you yet,' she said quietly. 'There is hope for that shepherd girl down there, more hope than she knows. There is more hope for all of us, more hope for the world than we could ever have dreamed of.'

'Look! The kingfisher again!' She pointed into the wadi, as the last shadows were driven away by the risen sun.

22 Ascension

‘ ‘‘Parting’’, they say, ‘‘is such sweet sorrow’’. But surely, Mary, when finally your son was taken from you, grief must have been piled on grief. You had lost him once already in death. One such loss is enough for anyone, and a death as terrible as his is too much for most. But you suffered a double bereavement. Resurrection, beyond the faintest hope, gave him back to you for a time. Ascension snatched him from you again, and that time the loss was final. You will live with it to your dying day. Where can any sweetness be in your sorrow?’

‘No, no! It was not like that at all,’ Mary replied. ‘There was no parting. Ascension means there can be no more parting, never, never. We just got over the shock of resurrection, that is all, and we began to see what it meant.

‘It had all seemed such a small affair. Oh, of course, the grief of his death had enveloped me entirely, and all of those who had been close to him. Yet, as we had taken him down, laboriously, from his cross, and hurried him to Joseph’s tomb, it had all seemed so insignificant. Not for us. Our worlds had been shattered. But the soldiers had gone back to their work, the city had settled down for the rhythms of the Sabbath and the memories of Passover, and the leopards and the owls had begun to stir for the hunt. Nothing, it seemed then, had changed. On our way to the tomb, we had seen no wolves living with lambs, no lions eating straw like the ox, no little children playing safely at the holes of asps. The earth had seemed entirely empty of the knowledge of the Lord.

'A few stories had been told, a few people healed. Others had become disturbed, fearful and angry, but they would soon recover their equilibrium. The world had already returned to normal. And we had dreamed such dreams! Our hopes had been so high, higher than Sinai, and brighter than the waters of Eden. Golgotha had taken them all away.

'So when they came flooding back so unexpectedly with the tall waters of resurrection behind them, you can imagine we were quite carried away. Where was this torrent taking us? We had pitched our tents in the dry wadi of the shadow of death, and thought the rains would never fall again. We were terrified. The waters carried us beyond desolation, beyond anything we had ever known. We had been tied up by grief, and were not ready for such freedom. We were like small children lost in a strange place, and wished only to return to where things were without hope, but at least were familiar and predictable.

'And then, through the sounds of our panic we caught the strains of his laughter, and knew it for certain this time as the laughter of God. We felt again his embrace, and in his arms found God's love.

'In truth we were being rolled along on the waves of God's merriment, and the morning stars were singing the "Alleluia Chorus", and the heavenly beings were shouting themselves hoarse with joy. But we did not realize that. The larger truth we could not take in at first. It still seemed only a small affair. The rest of the world went on its familiar way, and only we seemed aware that things had changed. But, if I am honest, it was not as simple as that. We were as preoccupied with our new

joy, as much as we had been with our pain. We were still
shut up in our little room, unaware of the deep swirl in
the ocean or the trembling of the air, deaf to the shaking
of the earth and the dancing in heaven. Our only thought
was that we had him back, and that was all we needed.
We had been full of death, and now we were bursting
with the liveliness of God, and that, we thought, was
enough. His resurrection had dispelled our grief and
brought us the surprise of joy, but otherwise it had not
yet changed us. We had not come to terms with it.

'Not until we went out, beyond the city walls again,
outside our upper room, beyond the cramped streets of
the old city, and climbed, as we had so many times with
him, the low ridge of the Mount of Olives. We looked
toward the Dead Sea, and saw on its shores meadows full
of flowers and woods of new-leafed trees. Crowning the
heights of the mountains on its far side was a great city,
shining gold in the sun. The colours of its precious stones
made an arc that tied heaven to earth. A carnival
procession was winding its way through the city's streets,
and the music of the angels' band came faintly to our ears.
You have never heard such jazz in all your born days! And
there he was! In the middle of the procession, riding on
the shoulders of Adam and Eve! They set him down in the
middle of a huge square, and we watched as God was
made complete again, and the Creator and the bright
Spirit took his pierced hands in theirs and danced. My
word, how the angels played then and how the people
cheered! And we cheered with them, and threw our hats
as high as heaven!

'We knew then that his death and resurrection had not
been small affairs at all. They did not belong to us for us
to keep. They belonged to all the world, to all creation,

to heaven and all eternity. We let them go, and they set us free. All was changed, and in due time all would be well. My son was home, and I would never lose him again. And so, you see, there was no parting. Ascension means there can be no more parting. Never. Never.'

23 *The Free Spirit of God*

Oh, black were the waters of the world's beginning! Black and wild, fathom-deep in fear. No gentle swell. No regular breathing of tides. No predictable currents. No Gulf Stream to bring future warmth to northern shores and let palm trees grow beside Scottish lochs. Just wild, capricious, dangerous chaos. Oh, black were the waters at the world's beginning, and black, too, jet-black the air that spanned their surface!

Through that dark flew the Spirit of God, small, with sharp, pointed wings, tilting from side to side, dipping into the troughs of the huge waves, sliding over their crests as they rose and broke apart. He flew back and forth, back and forth, weaving the ocean into currents, and calming the waters' fear, till eventually their breathing became easy, and he could rest awhile.

The world had begun.

Light was born, and showed a grey earth. The seas were calm now, but had no colour, and the land was but a series of shadows. The Spirit of God spread his wings, and, with his long tail rippling behind him like a bride's train, glided down till he came to land on the top of God's mountain. He puffed out his breast, and shook his tail into a huge fan. The bright feathers quivered, their many eyes holding the earth tight in their gaze. Thus God brought colour to the world's cheeks.

Light was born, the earth blushed with colour, yet still nothing could be heard. The waves of the seas broke

without a sound. The wind came and went as but a silent
breath upon the back of the world's neck. Neither the
sea, nor the air, nor any of the creatures of the new earth
had any voice.

So, in the middle of the desert, at the foot of the same
mountain, the Spirit of God dressed himself in brown,
crept into the middle of a thick bush, and set it ablaze
with his song. Thus God let creation speak.

When all was done, when all was good, when all was
very good, the Spirit of God refused to rest. Instead he
bent his strong wings to his body and fell to earth. At the
bottom of his fall, almost brushing the surface of the land,
he swung up again towards the sun, and twisting, turning,
tumbling, beating hard, then folding, falling once again,
he *flew*, flying for sheer joy, etching on the sky his
exuberance, and all God's grace and beauty.

Two men watched him. One raised a gun. 'No!' the
other cried. 'He'll be of no use to us shot to pieces. Leave
him be for now. Wait till he's finished showing off, then
we'll catch him when he's still.'

'What are you going to do with him?' asked the man
with the gun.

'Wait and see.'

'I haven't the time to wait and see,' said the first,
raised the gun and fired. He hit the Spirit through the
wing. The Spirit twisted one last time, and fell in agony
to the ground.

'Now look what you've done!'

'It's all right. I haven't killed him. Just snicked his
wing. It'll mend, I dare say, if we take him home with
us.'

So they put the Spirit of God in a sack, took him off
with them, and locked him in a cage. Word got around,

and people came from far and wide to see what they had got. They came to look and prod. They goaded him to see if he might bite. They called him 'Pretty Joey' in silly voices to make him talk. They went away disappointed, and returned to their pigeons and their budgerigars.

One day someone called to see him, who did not prod, nor goad, nor put on a silly voice. He simply stood for a long time in front of the cage gazing at him.

'How much do you want for him?' he asked the two men.

'Not for sale,' said one.

'One hundred,' said the other.

'Ten,' replied the stranger.

'Ten! Fifty.'

'Twenty.'

'Forty.'

'Thirty.'

'Done.'

And so, for thirty pieces of silver the stranger picked up the cage and took the Spirit of God away with him in the boot of his car.

He drove straight to the new church. The people were gathered for worship. He flung open the doors, and shouted, right in the middle of the prayers, 'Look what I've got!'

The cage was not good enough, of course. It was an ugly, hotchpotch affair. So they made a larger one of special beauty, with gold and silver bars, and hung it high above the altar. They erected a large sign outside the building. 'We have the Spirit of God!' it proclaimed. 'Come and join us!' And people did, till the church was too small, and they had to build another, with an even more splendid cage, suspended from the ledge beneath the east window by a heavy silver chain.

One evening, the day before the tenth anniversary of the Spirit's arrival, when a great celebration would be held, a small boy climbed carefully down the chain. He had hidden behind a pile of chairs when they were locking the doors. He eased himself on to the top of the cage, and then, locking his feet round the last few links of the chain, he leant over till he could reach the catch on the cage's door. It was stiff. It had not been opened since first the cage was hung in the church. He stretched out a little further, his heart beating wildly. The catch suddenly gave way, and the door swung sharply open. He almost lost his grip and fell, but somehow he managed to twist his body upright, and scrambled back up the chain and on to the ledge. He scampered along the triforium till he came to the spiral staircase. He hurled himself down it and fell out of the door at the bottom. Picking himself up, he ran as fast as he could to the west doors. He had put the huge key in the lock already. With both hands he turned it, and pushed the doors open as far as they would go. The Spirit of God touched him lightly with the tip of his wing as he flew out into the dark.

The boy watched him as he tumbled high across the moon and stars, and listened entranced as he filled all heaven with his song. Behind him, at the far end of the building, the empty cage swung on its silver chain.

24 ~ Find God, for God's Sake!

The old man lay in his bed, waiting for God. He was not a religious man. Never had been. He still did not feel the need for any religion. But he did feel the need for God. He wanted to find God before he died. His search was a terrifyingly empty one. He tried to remember a few prayers, but the words did not come out right. He let them out into the silence of the night, but they did not return to him. He closed his eyes, and tried to conjure God up in his imagination, but no pictures came. It was not as easy as he thought. Perhaps that was a good thing. For if God did come to him, what would he be like? Would he be like that crazy teacher at his school all those years ago who had caned him whenever he had done something wrong, and had sometimes caned him harder when he had done nothing at all? Even his homework had come back with the marks of the birch upon it. Had the teacher taken the school birch home specially, or had he kept a separate one handy in the corner of his sitting-room? He had always wondered that. He had never forgotten that birch, nor the teacher's expression when he had used it on him in class. Would God come with a birch in his hand? Better not come at all, then. But then the dreadful emptiness would engulf him once again, and he would cry out for God to appear, just once, just for a moment, just so that he would know, and could die knowing. Whether for better or for worse, he had to know the truth.

He had never felt so lonely in all his life. But you would not have thought it of him. People were constantly popping in on him, and the young woman who lived next door had done his shopping for years, and was still doing it, as well as his cooking and cleaning and washing. At first he had thanked her, but as time had gone on and he had become more turned in on himself, he had come to take her for granted. Then he had learned he could take it out on her with impunity, and so he had, till he had come to despise her. It had not helped her that she was Jewish.

It did not occur to him to ask her to find God for him, but one day, when the blackness of God's absence was more fearful than usual, he decided to send his friends to search him out and bring him word of what they found. 'Don't come back, till you find him,' he told them. 'But when you do, if you do, come and tell me.'

So they went out one by one into God's world, to look for its Creator, while the young Jewish woman continued to look after the old man and supply him with his daily bread. Eventually his friends returned and told him of their discoveries.

'I have found her fearful beauty,' said the first. 'I went down to the meadows near the river, as it was getting towards dusk. I saw a white bird flying slowly above the grasses and meadow flowers. At first I thought it was a gull, but when it turned in my direction and came closer, I saw it was an owl, a white owl. It was hunting for food for its young, flying slowly, low above the ground, near the level of my own eyes. It came straight for me, its ears and eyes and every muscle of its body, every feather of its quiet wings gathered to the task of the hunt. For a long moment I looked that owl in the eye. Large, shining black, perfectly round and deeper than the ocean were that owl's eyes, and I tell you they pierced my soul. God searched me out and knew me in those eyes, and I understand now how great, how very fearful her beauty is.'

'It was late one summer's evening,' the second one said. 'The sky was dark with thunder, and before I reached the place the rain fell noisily and hid the hills and fields beneath its folds. I had to take shelter for a space, but the lightning retreated over the horizon, the rain became more gentle, and I took the path to the hide overlooking the small pool among the reeds. I was quite alone. The families had all gone home hours before, and no one else had thought to come out in such a storm. I raised the wooden flaps in the hide and looked out across the pool. Nothing. I had come all that way. The light was fading and I was wet. I had come all that way. The rain beat harder on the wooden roof and made its predictable patterns on the disc of the pool. My heart sank. And then, as I was wondering how long I would stay, the creature's head broke the surface of the water, just yards in front of me. It was playing. Round and round it went in tight circles, diving and resurfacing continuously, arching its broad back and churning the water with its tail. I caught its bright eyes and the sharpness of its teeth. That otter was entirely, quite entirely in its element, and showed me the child in God, his playfulness and sheer unadulterated glee.'

'And I,' said a third, 'saw mountain flowers bent in the wind and the rain, and saw a single leaf hanging on the branch of a late autumn tree, and found again the smallness, the fragility, the unobtrusiveness, the quiet vulnerability of God.'

'You didn't find him round here, then,' said the old

man impatiently. 'You with your owls and your otters and your flowers and leaves! I don't live in the woods, or on the hills, or by the river, or among the reeds. I live *here*, in these grey streets. Are you telling me I will never find him here? If that is what you mean, then I wish I hadn't asked you to search him out!'

'Oh no!' they cried. 'We stumbled upon God beyond the town first, it is true, and perhaps that is no accident, for here we can so easily miss her, or crowd him out in our busyness. But we have found God in these very streets, also. Have you seen that old couple across the road? Have you watched how they care for one another? It has become a habit with them, a habit of over fifty years. They do not notice their gentleness, though it tells of the very gentleness of God, and of his stamina and of that persistent love for which he is so famous. Have you not seen them? And have you not noticed that young man who lives in the studio of the old sculptor the other side of the river and helps him in his work? Have you seen their sculptures? They dream of changing the world, those two, and so they do! To live with the figures they produce is to find a corner of the kingdom of God. They show us God's exuberance, the extravagance, the prodigality of his inventiveness!'

'Sounds to me all they've shown you is how to string a whole lot of long words together,' the old man muttered.

'Or,' said the friends, ignoring him, 'have you seen the anger of the black woman round the corner, whose son got beaten up the other day on his way back from school? Have you heard her cries? Have you heard her shouts? Have you listened to her hurt and her bewilderment? They do not know if her son will live or die, and nor does she. She will show you what you need to know of the anger and the bewilderment of God. And the men who hang around the street corners with nothing to do will remind you of them also and his passion for justice, and the men and women in that ugly place by the river where you worked years ago, and where they are trying so hard to rediscover their common humanity in the midst of it all, they will give you a glimpse of the creativity and compassion of God.'

'But I don't work there any more!' shouted the old man. 'I haven't worked there for years, ever since I had the accident and I've been like this. What about my wife's grave? Did you go there? It was the only place her cancer could find for her. Did you go *there*? And did you read the headstone right next to hers, and see how young he was when he died? Our only child, and he died for no reason. Eighteen months. *Eighteen months*! Did you read the dates on his tombstone? No, of course, you didn't! Get out, and leave me in peace! Come on, woman, I've been lying like this for too long. Sit me up, and then go and get my tea!'

The young Jewish woman had been in the room all the time, watching the old man, but the friends had not noticed her, nor given her a thought. She slipped down the stairs to the kitchen and cooked the man's meal. Twice during her preparations he banged his stick on the floorboards, and she had to go up to find out what he wanted. He was only wondering where his food was and why she was taking so long. After half an hour or so she climbed the stairs towards his room, carrying his tray.

She could hear his sobbing before she got to the door. She pushed it open and put the tray down on the chest of drawers. He was sitting up against his pillows shaking with grief. He was crying for his wife who was dead. He was crying for his son who was dead. He was crying for himself, knowing that his own death was at hand. The woman came towards him, and he looked at her through his tears.

He looked straight at her, and for the first time for years he saw her, and then as she held him tight in her arms, he discovered for the first time the love of God and felt her embrace. It was a long moment. Eventually, against the slow ticking of the clock, the woman released him and closed his eyes. His tears had stopped flowing. He was dead. His God, trembling, her cheeks wet with her own tears as well as those of the old man she loved so, picked up the tray and slowly went downstairs.

25   *The Great Fish*

The sea lay back upon its bed and closed its eyes. From the top of the cliff the slow rise and fall of its breathing was quite imperceptible. It had spent its energies in the storm of the previous night. Insects hummed over the gorse and heather. A buzzard spun tall circles in the sky, and only the gulls were noisy. A large pyramid of rock stood out from the base of the cliff. The herring-gulls had it for their kingdom, and were loudly proclaiming their sovereignty.

Then, all of a sudden, just out from the stack, something broke the surface of the water. Some of the gulls at once went to investigate. By the time they reached the spot it had gone, the waters had closed again, and only a few jagged rings of foam were left

The birds flew back to their rock and turned their minds to other things. The buzzard rose still higher, its wings spread wide to the warm air, and was now scarcely visible from the ground. Certainly, the couple so seriously walking the cliff path did not see it. They were too busy concentrating on where to put their feet.

They reached a particularly treacherous stretch of the path, when behind them the great fish surfaced again. With slow power and unutterable grace it bent its huge back out of the water, to catch for a moment the heat of the sun. Only for a moment. The curve of its body took it out of sight once more, and the two people on the path, still watching their steps on the cliff's edge, saw nothing, nor caught the small sounds of its disturbance.

A few yards more, and surely it would rise again. And so it did, and again and again, till its course took it round the end of the headland, and the fall of the cliff blocked my view.

I stood transfixed, unable and quite unwilling to move. Beneath my feet the earth trembled, while high, very high above me the buzzard made one last circle, closed its wings, and swung down in a series of loops that took the angels' breath away. My eyes were focused still on the sea, upon its smooth, unruffled surface, upon its now perceptible, slow swell. I was watching for the fish to appear just once more, to leap in one majestic leap, perhaps, and show me the full extent of its glory.

'Do you still want more?' a voice enquired. 'Was that not sufficient? He has done more than enough, surely, for one day, for one year, for one lifetime, if you will but remember.'

I had not seen her coming. She stood beside me, looking out beyond the headland. She turned her head and smiled. 'If you want him so, he will show himself again, before the sun sinks and the gulls fall silent for the night. But you must not expect any leaps. You cannot have all his splendour yet.'

She pointed far out to sea, and as she did so the waters parted and the curve of the fish showed again, etching its lines upon my brain and deep-warming my heart.

'This is a holy place,' I murmured.

'Our Mount Sinai,' she replied, 'and this our cleft in its rock.'

Behind us the gorse caught the fire of the setting sun and burned bright gold.

'He will go deep now,' she continued. 'He will seek again the dark recesses of the world's mind, and take there his strength, his beauty and his unassuming grace. He will swim in the very deepest depths, where we might imagine there is no chance of life. He will go deeper than any fear, than any hurt or hate, deeper than oblivion. The ocean loves him and lets him roam free. He curves and bends within her, while she hurls her delight against the rocks and roars her pleasure for us to hear. Yet her song, the ocean's ancient, unending song, is but an echo of his. Out there beyond the farthest horizon, he will join his humpback whales and sing with them the symphony of his creation. And when he sings, the angels will pause from their dance, and the stars will bend their light to listen.

'And what will we do? What will *we* do?' Her voice changed to a harsh and fearful regret. '*We* will sharpen our harpoons! Look!'

She pointed down to the spot below us where first I had seen the fish.

'Look!'

The foam that had broken upon his back could yet be seen, still spreading in wide circles upon the dark surface of the waters. It was the red of blood.

'This is not only our Sinai,' she said. 'It is his Golgotha!'

26 *Whispering Voices, and an Ancient Wood*

'What a beautiful baby!' they said when she was born. 'What a lively child!' they declared, while she still was a child. They loved her mischief then, when she could, as they thought, do no harm by it. They indulged her then. When, however, she grew to be a woman, they became distrustful of her daring, and were soon alarmed by it.

She lived in a small, self-important town, where people knew who was who and what was what, and taught its children to obey its narrow proprieties. She was not well taught, or else had too much of a will of her own. She was altogether too adventurous, too plain in her speaking. She was, for that town, too individual, altogether.

Her name was mentioned at a meeting of the Town Council. They decided to put a stop to her. They allowed her to put her case, but they did not listen, or else did not understand. Some people said the charges against her were trumped up for political reasons, but that only made the councillors draw closer together, close ranks, and close minds against her.

'We will put a stop to you,' they told her.

'You cannot change the way I am,' she replied.

'Oh yes, we can,' they said. 'We can wear you down. We can stretch your spirit to breaking point, and then break it. We can curb your liking for adventure, and destroy it. We can convince you that you are in the wrong. We can load the blame on to your shoulders, and make you bear it. We can make you think you deserve what is coming to you. You know the score. Someone is abused, or raped, and who do they blame but themselves! It is often the way of things. Such perversity! But there it is, and we will take advantage of it. We will not abuse you, of course, nor rape you, not physically, at least. Nothing so sordid. We will simply malign you, and turn a deaf ear to your complaints. That should do it.'

'But you cannot alter my vision,' she said defiantly.

'Oh yes, we can!' they cried. 'Oh yes, we can! We will wear you down till you think our small world is the only one there is. You will come to our small town ways, by and by. Your "vision", as you call it, will seem so extravagant, your adventures so imprudent, so foolish. You will learn our self-important ways, because you will come to think they are the only ways there are to learn. You will learn them to survive. You will come to play our games, by and by, see things as we see them, think there is nothing else to think. You will bow yourself down before our realities. One day you will be as we are. We will make sure of that. After all, we are good men, most of us, doing our best for the town. Times are hard, and it is all we can do to keep this town's head above water. We have to keep the ship afloat (you won't mind us mixing our metaphors), and the crew happy. If we cannot achieve that, then at least we must try to prevent a mutiny. You must understand that. If you were in our position, you would understand only too well. Ours is what they call "the real world", you see. Our job is a hard one. It is not easy being councillors in this place. You must understand that. People expect so much of us. We need your sympathy, deserve your gratitude and your loyalty. We are good men, after all, doing our best. We understand how things are, and how they must be. It is as simple as that. We will do what we can to help you appreciate that. That is all. Thank you.'

She left the Council chamber and walked the narrow streets of the town. The voices of the councillors kept her company. 'That is all,' they whispered. 'This is how it is.'

Beyond the town, a few miles to the west, she came to a railway line. Beyond it a narrow road kept to the bottom of a valley and led towards an ancient wood. To its left the valley's side rose too steeply for the plough, and at the right time of year was yellow with cowslips. On to the top of that ridge and along it into the wood wound a track, grooved into the land by centuries of feet and hooves, lending the landscape a little elegance with its curves. It was far too early for the cowslips, and the track was thick, sucking-sweet in mud. Near the top of its climb someone had put a bench. A simple affair. Nothing to say who had placed it there. But there it was, overlooking the valley and, in the spring, its cowslips.

It was too misty for the view, but the woman sat down there, nevertheless. The mist seemed to have got thicker. She could see nothing. 'That is all. This is how it is,' the voices whispered. 'Play our game. Bow to our realities. Our proprieties are not so narrow, when you look at them from our point of view. We know how it is. Look! You can see nothing! That's how it is! See? This is all! This is all there is!'

She got up from the bench. The mud had turned to lead on her shoes, and great splashes of it were hardening on her legs, but undeterred she walked on up the track towards the edge of the wood.

The wood had been there long, long before the town. The wood had always been there, long before human beings came to walk the earth and carve their tracks upon it. The wood was unaware of the streets of the town. It did not observe the town's proprieties, nor see things as the town saw them. It lived a life of its own. It had known through many millennia all sorts of adventures. It had its own quiet daring. Though at that time of year it seemed dead or dying, its decay was quite illusory. Its decay was the very stuff of its life. Beneath the litter of last year's leaves life waited to show itself, and already some of the smaller trees had draped themselves with folds of catkins and thus told of the delicacy of the coming spring.

The catkins did not move. The wood lay very still. Curving to the right the track dipped and rounded the top of a small coomb. She stopped and looked, vaguely aware of the rough pasture slipping sharply away. As she did so, the mist curled its way up the sides of the valley towards her, then quickly folded itself away and disappeared. The long shadows of a new winter sun stretched beneath her. In the far distance she could see the town from which she had come. A breeze blew gently after the mist and made the catkins dance and shimmer in the sun. High above the trees a buzzard soared in the bright air, and its mewing reached her as she stood in the sweet mud. She looked up. The bird had lived in the wood long before the town was built. Truth to tell, it had always lived there. It had soared above that valley for millennia, before ever the track was made along its edge. Its mewing call was far older than the town, and hearing it, the woman thought how very small the town looked.

Again the bird called, and now it filled her hearing. The whispering voices had gone. All she could hear was the cry of the bird, and the ancient wood shifting gently in the breeze.

She looked at the town. 'Damn you!' she cried. High above her the buzzard rolled and turned, rolled again quite on to its back, then, bending its wings close to its body, dived headlong towards the trees.

The woman's heart danced. She was free! *This* was how it was!

27 A Crucifixion
in Heaven

He was young, tall and strong, good-looking, too. But one
thing he knew, and knew very well. He was no good.
People had been telling him that for years.

It started with his Dad when he was small. His Dad got
in the habit of coming home drunk late at night, and when
he stopped hitting his Mum, he would come into his
bedroom and start on him. Night after night he lay in his
small bed with the bedclothes pulled over him, dreading
the sound of his father coming down the street. He would
hear him shouting and swearing before he got within a
hundred yards of the front door. He would hear him slam
the door, and lurch heavily up the stairs. He would put
his hands over his ears to try to block out his mother's
screams, and then he would hear the crash of his own
door as it was flung open. He used to cower under the
bedclothes at the foot of the bed, but it was no use. His
Dad always found him.

Twice his Dad nearly killed him. The second time he
was in hospital for several weeks. Of course, it was his
own fault. His Dad could not help it. It was something
wrong with him, something terribly wrong. Why else
would his Dad hit him so hard? He was no good. It was his
fault when his Dad got put in prison for nearly killing his
Mum. It was obviously his fault when his Mum got cross
with him for wetting the bed. His Mum loved him in her
way, but she did not know how to show it very well, and

he did not see it when she did. He was a bad boy, so why should anyone love him?

He went to school when he was five, but they soon declared he was out of hand. They could do nothing with him. They could not teach him anything. All they could do was try to keep him from bullying the other children, or spoiling their work. He was not stupid, but he thought he must be, because he could not manage what the other children were beginning to do.

You can guess what he was like when he was older. He took cars, drugs and girls, not always in that order, sometimes all at once. The girls did not stay with him for long. He hit them about too much. He thought that was what you did with women. By a miracle one girl fell in love with him and said so, and eventually he started to believe her, though he did not understand what he was believing.

But then he took her out for a spin one dark November night. He had never driven an Aston Martin before. He had never come across one, not with the keys left in the ignition. He did not know what it could do, but he told his girlfriend he would find out. He did. When they reached the edge of the town, already going at sixty, he put his foot hard down. They could not take the corner, not at that speed. They hit the tree at one hundred and ten miles an hour. The girl was lucky. He was not.

And that is how, for the first time in his life, at least the first time he could think of, he met God.

He looked him up and down for a long time. 'You bastard!' he said. 'Where have you been all this time? Bloody nowhere! Bloody useless, you are! Call yourself God! I'll turn you into a God! Come on, God, let's make you look the part! I've got all the gear!'

He dressed God in a purple robe, put a crown of long thorns on his head, lashed a beam of wood across his shoulders, and whipped him through the streets of the heavenly Jerusalem, shouting at him at the top of his voice. The streets were silent, but for his abuse. The angels hid their faces and covered them with their wings, and the other inhabitants of the city stood stock still, their heads bowed in grief, as their God and his tormentor passed them by. The flowers covering the roads closed their petals, the birds stopped singing, and the fountains ceased to play. In the middle of the city the little procession came to a halt, and there the young man completed his act of vengeance.

He stood back to admire his handiwork. Behind him the angels and the people of the city and the other creatures of heaven waited. He had done a good job. He turned on his heel and left.

Leaving, however, was not as straightforward as he expected. The crucified God kept returning to his mind, drawing him back to where the crowd watched and waited. At the third attempt to escape the young man got as far as the edge of the city, but then he hesitated, turned again, walked back along the empty streets, and slipped into the back of the crowd, hoping not to be noticed.

'Take him down,' said an angel at his shoulder. 'Take him down. You have done enough.'

He looked at the cross. 'Do you see what you have done?' the angel enquired.

For the first time he did. He had not nailed God on that cross, but himself and his father. Till that moment he did not know how much he hated them both. Yet he *had* put God there. He had put *God* there! The pain was God's pain now, and he was carrying the hatred and the despair.

'Take him down,' the angel repeated quietly. 'You have seen enough.'

He moved through the crowd, went up to the cross, pulled out the nails, removed the thorns, took his God down and laid him gently in his lap.

'Welcome home,' the angel said.

28 At the Dawn
of Heaven

Heaven's dawn marbled the flat surface of the lake with soft blues, greys, pinks and golds. God sat on the rocks, waiting. Far behind her, too far to disturb her peace, were the towers and spires of the New Jerusalem, the Heavenly City, as light as angels' wings, and just as beautiful. God had come to get away from it all.

A line was being drawn across the water towards her. It was her friend the otter, swimming with his head held high and his bright eyes shining. The animal clambered on to the rocks, shook himself, and settled down.

'Getting you down, again?' he enquired.

God smiled. 'It's good to be here with you,' she said.

'Come for a swim?'

'Why not?' replied God, and gave the otter a mischievous grin.

Now you might have thought that God, the great God of the universe, the maker of the whale and the porpoise, the flying fish, the gannet and the tern, and the otter too, for that matter, you might have thought that such a God would have dived, with an elegance and grace beyond compare, and with not a splash to be heard or seen. But I tell you God *jumped*, and with such a jump, that she shot all the creatures swimming peacefully in that heavenly lake out of the water and sent them spiralling tens of feet into the air.

'Typical!' yelled the otter as he hurtled upwards, and 'Alleluuuuuuuuuuuia!' as he tumbled down. He hit the water with a mighty splash. After that all was heavenly mayhem, as the creatures of the lake of heaven were caught up in God's play. The birds flying above it, the flowers and trees round its edge and of its islands, the water itself, the air, the ground and the rock, these also became part of the general delight, that delight that accompanied their God wherever she went, and which, that dawn, had taken such an extravagantly rumbustious form.

The noise of it all reached the city, and made its human inhabitants wonder what in heaven was going on. The angels knew, of course. They had heard it all before. They had been part of God's games since before the world was made. Soon, they knew, God would start behaving herself again, and things would quieten down.

And so they did. The lake sank back to its former calm, and now two lines were being drawn across its surface, one beside the other. God and the otter climbed on to the rock. They were silent for a long time. The otter waited for his companion to speak. He was in no hurry. (There is no hurry in heaven. It is one of the heavenly things about heaven.)

God shook the beauty of the lake out of her eyes. 'I only wish they wouldn't take me so very seriously,' she said, 'those human beings back in the city. Most of them don't know how to take me, you know.'

The otter remembered being hurled into the air by God's jumping into the water. 'I'm not surprised,' he said.

God gave him a shove, and laughed. 'But I am so far from what they expect.'

'The angels tell me you've been playing hoop-la with people's haloes again.'

'Of course.'

'And that the spires of the city are festooned with

them, and people can't get them down, and you've told the angels not to help.'

'Certainly. Does them good to be without them for a bit.'

'And you think they expect you to behave like that?'

'Well, some of them. The children do, of course. They get the hang of things straightaway. We have a marvellous time together. They're nearly as good as otters,' and God laughed again and gave her friend another shove, so hard that this time he fell off the rock. He climbed out again and shook himself vigorously, right in God's face. The drops of water went flying bright gold into all the air.

'Another swim?'

'Not yet.' There was silence between them for another spell. 'Do you know, they are *afraid* of me. Afraid of *me*! Can you imagine? They daren't look me in the face. They get straight down on their knees, and there they stay. Or else, they turn their backs on me, or try to find somewhere to hide. Why such fear of me? Where, my friend, does it come from? You've never been afraid of me. These rocks have never been afraid of me, nor the flowers here. Why should they not know what you all know? I thought I had made them especially wise. I thought I had shared with them all the secrets of my heart, and had taken particular trouble to come out into the open and show them what I was like. Why then are they so afraid of me?'

'Because,' said the otter, 'they have made you in their own image, and in the image of those of their own kind they fear the most. They have made you into a great king, and even with the most benevolent of their rulers they are on their best behaviour. With the tyrannical they are scared to death. Sometimes I have heard them speak of you, and though their words have not made you into the very worst they know, they have not made you into their best either. That is why they are afraid.'

'But that is idolatry, to make me in their own image.'

'Exactly.'

'Is that why they praise me all the time?'

'Of course.'

'*You* don't praise me all the time.'

'That's why you keep coming out here to sit on the rock and talk.'

'One of the reasons, my friend, yes.' God paused. 'So what can I do?'

'Keep throwing their haloes on to the spires. And get the children to help. I remember you telling them they would have to become like children to keep your company. Well, you and the children can show them what that means. After all, *you've* never grown up.'

God roared with laughter.

'And bring them here for a swim, and do your jumping-in act. That would show them! Catch them up in your delight, when they're not expecting it. Send them high in the air on your pleasure, and let them splash down into your mischief. Perhaps after that they would dare face you. They do so need to find the courage to do that.'

'Does it really require *courage*?'

'Of course not. But they think it does, so for them it does.'

'Do you think it would work?'

'It just might.' The otter grinned.

'Do you think we need another practice?'

'Certainly.'

'We'll jump together this time. Let's wake the dead!' And so they did.